US
WA...
& AUXILIARIES

INCLUDING US COAST GUARD

USS Freedom

AUTHOR'S NOTES

It has been four years since the first edition of *US Navy Warships & Auxiliaries* was published and in those intervening years I have recieved much encouragement and feedback from readers - so much so that this updated and expanded Second Edition has been produced.

One of the recurring themes from feedback were requests to include the US Coast Guard within the book. Initially I dismissed this as the intention was to produce a pocket guide and it was difficult to see how I could include yet another service and still keep the book to a reasonable size. However, in June 2010, whilst in Canada and the USA, I was fortunate enough to meet James T. Flynn, a retired USNR Chief Hospital Corpsman - and USCG officianado - who was also keen to see the USCG included. In fact, having seen the ommission of the USCG from the First Edition, he produced his own USCG 'supplement'. Using Jim's book as a guide, and with e-mail updates, this expanded Second Edition includes an additional 48 pages covering the ships and aircraft of the USCG.

Researching such a vast topic as this is never easy, and though the USN, Military Sealift Command and the USCG have extensive and informative websites, the information contained on them can only be as current as the last update. In trying to iron out some of the conflicting information I have been most fortunate to have had the seemingly endless help and support from numerous Public Affairs Offices, for whom, it would seem, no request is too difficult. My thanks go out to them.

I would also like to acknowledge the work of the photographers of both the military and naval shipbuilders whose photographs bring this book to life. I have drawn extensively on their images, without which this volume would be a dry list of technical information. Where known, individuals are credited alongside each image.

This book can only be as up to date as the day it was printed, but any errors which may have crept in are solely my own, and I would be grateful to be made aware of any so that they can be updated in any future editions. Contact me at warshipworld@navy-books.com

Steve Bush
Cornwall, December 2010

THE UNITED STATES NAVY

The United States Navy has a large global footprint, operating in almost every ocean of the world. It comprises six active numbered fleets - The Second Fleet currently oversees 126 ships homeported at US Navy installations along the East Coast of the USA with responsibilities for operations in the Atlantic Ocean and the Arctic.

The Third Fleet's area of responsibility includes approximately fifty million square miles of the eastern and northern Pacific ocean areas including the Bering Sea, Alaska, the Aleutian Islands and a sector of the Arctic. Major oil and trade sea lines of communication within this area are critically important to the economic health of the United States and friendly nations throughout the Pacific Rim region. Third Fleet HQ is at San Diego.

The Fifth Fleet is responsible for naval forces in the Persian Gulf, Red Sea, Arabian Sea, and the coast off East Africa as far south as Kenya. It shares a commander and headquarters with US Naval Forces Central Command (NAVCENT).

The Sixth Fleet is the USN's operational unit and staff of United States Naval Forces Europe, and once had its own headquarters in Gaeta, Italy. USS MOUNT WHITNEY is the Sixth Fleet flagship based at Gaeta and operating in the Mediterranean Sea.

The Seventh Fleet is the USN's permanent forward projection force based in Yokosuka, Japan, with units positioned near South Korea and Japan. It is a component fleet force under the United States Pacific Fleet. At present it is the largest of the forward-deployed US fleets, with 50 - 60 ships, 350 aircraft and 60,000 Navy and Marine Corps personnel.

The Fourth Fleet was re-established in the summer of 2008 and is a major command of the USN in the South Atlantic, operating as a component of the joint US Southern Command whose aim will be to assist in counter narcotics operations, humanitarian and goodwill interventions, and joint training with regional security partners

In 2010 a further numbered fleet was stood up, but its function is primarily shore-based. The Tenth Fleet is based at Fort Meade, Maryland and is the Naval component to US Cyber Command, the sub-unified cyber commander. As such it provides operational support to Navy commanders worldwide, supporting information, computer, electronic warfare and space operations. In addition to joint and service reporting, the command also serves as the Navy's cryptologic commander, reporting to the Central Security Service. Tenth Fleet has operational control over Navy information, computer, cryptologic, and space forces.

Having described the fleet structure it is worthwhile having a look at the US Navy mission and the ships available to conduct such operations. The mission of the US Navy is to maintain, train and equip combat-ready Naval forces capable of winning wars, deterring aggression and maintaining freedom of the seas.

Few can argue that the US Navy of 2010 is ably equipped to conduct such tasks - indeed with a deployable battle force of 288 ships there is no one country that can match their maritime power (indeed if you take the next thirteen largest navies by tonnage, it would still be hard to match the USN) - but a look at the statistics will show that, despite the number of ships available, the USN is being worked very hard. On a given day in 2010 the US Navy had 160 ships underway from their homeports (56% of total) of which 114 were deployed on operations (40%). It is a similar story for submarines with 29 attack submarines away from port (53%) of which 20 boats (37%) were on deployment. A more normal roulement cycle would be 33% of vessels deployed allowing the remaining 66% to be working up for deployment or being maintained having returned. This high usage rate is sure to impact on availability in coming years as these complex vessels require more and more time alongside to keep them maintained and operational. Key to keeping the fleet viable is a programme of replacement and modernisation. Most areas of naval warfare within the USN are undergoing a transition from old "cold war" generation vessles, to newer more flexible vessels whose capabilities are more pertinent to the operations of the 21st Century.

The long running Nimitz aircraft carrier construction programme has now come to an end with the delivery and acceptance of the tenth vessel, GEORGE BUSH. The carrier fleet now numbers eleven ships and is now all nuclear powered (with the final conventional ship KITTY HAWK paying off in 2009). The oldest of the ships ENTERPRISE, 50 years old in 2011, will be replaced by the new generation USS GERALD FORD in 2015. This new class of carrier will provide the Navy with a more capable ship with reduced weight to allow for future technology upgrades, increased sortie generation capability, 2.5 times more electrical power and reduced cost. The ships have been redesigned from the Nimitz class. They have the same hull lines and the same number of decks as a Nimitz-class carrier, but the footprint of the general arrangement has been totally rearranged to accommodate a new technology and meet all of the Navy's operational requirements and the aim is to reduce manning by 500-1200 thereby reducing the operating costs.

The Virginia class attack submarine programme is progressing and they are slowly replacing the ageing Los Angeles class submarines, seventeen of which (from a total of 62) have already been decommissioned. Designed as a cheaper alternative to the Seawolf class (perhaps up to £0.75 billion less per boat) they are a strange mixture of both controversy and success. There have been incidents of faulty welding and poor inspection routines for welding work which has resulted in the need to inspect, recertify, and in some cases, rework previous welds. More recently there have been instances of the anechoic hull covering, applied to absorb sonar and dampen radiated noise, delaminating from the hull. The welding issues seem to have been overcome, and the two companies building the boats are showing that they are able to deliver on cost and on time (in fact earlier in some cases).

The workhorses of the fleet are the cruisers, destroyers and frigates and there is much work being done to improve the USN's capability in these areas. Over the next several years, 22 Ticonderoga-class guided-missile cruisers and 62 Arleigh Burke-class guided-missile destroyers will undergo a structured modernisation to ensure they reach their projected 30 year service life. The ships will be fitted with new software, combat systems and machinery upgrades to improve all areas of ship functionality. The first ships to start receiving upgrades are the Ticonderoga-class cruisers: the first two of which, BUNKER HILL and MOBILE BAY have successfully completed modernisation.

Destroyer modernisation, beginning in late 2010, will mark the first time a major modernisation programme has begun while the remaining ships of the class are still being constructed. The first Arleigh Burke destroyers were built almost 20 years ago, and more advanced technologies are being built into the newer ships that will need to be backfitted into the older hulls.

The future cruiser programme has been cancelled and the ambitious Zumwalt destroyer programme scaled back to just three vessels in favour of extending the Arleigh Burke class production line. The multi-mission Zumwalt class is tailored for sustained operations in the littorals and land attack, and will provide independent forward presence and deterrence, support special operations forces, and operate as an integral part of joint and combined expeditionary forces. This futuristic looking vessel, designed with stealth in mind, was laid down in 2009.

The Navy has ambitions to increase in size to 313 ships and the key to this increase rests with the Littoral Combat Ship (LCS), effectively a replacement for the FFG 7 class frigates, but designed to incorporate modular mission modules, thereby creating a jack-of-all trades. However, what was envisaged as a cheap, multi-mission platform, has in practice turned out to be very expensive with many voicing concerns over whether the ship will ever achieve full operational capability across the wide spectrum of warfare functions envisaged for it. Two competing designs have been built; one a conventional single hulled vessel led by Lockheed Martin and the other a radical trimaran design by a team led by General Dynamics. It was thought that a decision on the winning design would have been made by the time we went to press but there is no sign of an announcement. Indeed the geographical distances between the two competing yards could possibly turn the debate into a political battle for jobs in the south or the north with strong lobbying from politicians in both areas. Add to that the track record in shipbuilding from the two competing consortia. Lockheed Martin have a proven track record, but the tempatation for the new kid on the block with the radical design to undercut their rival's bid could make this a very messy battle. With the Navy desperate to replace its elderly frigates and with a requirement for up to 50 of these new vessels, it is hoped that an early resolution is reached so that the programme can proceed.

The Navy is making big strides in its effort to replace elderly Amphibious tonnage, with several new programmes underway. The last of the Wasp class, MAKIN ISLAND is now in service, introducing gas turbine technology to the class vice the older steam plants. The new generation LHA 6 (or AMERICA class) builds on the experience of MAKIN ISLAND and the previous big deck amphibious ships, but these will be optimised for aircraft operations, primarily the F-35B Lightning II and Osprey. By doing away with the dock for landing craft in the stern the additional space can be utilised for an enlarged hangar deck, realignment and expansion of the aviation maintenance facilities, a significant increase in available stowage for parts and support equipment, and increased aviation fuel capacity.

The San Antonio class LPD programme continues to deliver ships and long lead items are now being acquired for the eleventh vessel. However, the class has been dogged by continuing reports of poor workmanship and unreliable machinery. It is hard to shrug off a bad reputation, but each successive ship in service is receiving fewer discrepancy cards during sea trials indicating that these concerns may at last have been overcome.

The next few years are going to be significant for the US Navy as it struggles to fight issues of obsolescence, while at the same time maintaining a high tempo of operations. If it wants to continue to have a global presence it needs to get a tight rein on the raft of new ship programmes so that the new technologies are brought forward into fleet service in a timely manner, to budget and, most importantly, constructed to a standard whereby reliability does not become an issue.

SHIPS OF THE UNITED STATES NAVY
Pennant Numbers

Ship	Pennant Number	Ship	Pennant Number
Aircraft Carriers		CHICAGO	SSN 721
		KEY WEST	SSN 722
ENTERPRISE	CVN 65	OKLAHOMA CITY	SSN 723
NIMITZ	CVN 68	LOUISVILLE	SSN 724
DWIGHT D. EISENHOWER	CVN 69	HELENA	SSN 725
CARL VINSON	CVN 70	OHIO	SSGN 726
THEODORE ROOSEVELT	CVN 71	MICHIGAN	SSGN 727
ABRAHAM LINCOLN	CVN 72	FLORIDA	SSGN 728
GEORGE WASHINGTON	CVN 73	GEORGIA	SSGN 729
JOHN C. STENNIS	CVN 74	HENRY M. JACKSON	SSBN 730
HARRY S. TRUMAN	CVN 75	ALABAMA	SSBN 731
RONALD REAGAN	CVN 76	ALASKA	SSBN 732
GEORGE H.W. BUSH	CVN 77	NEVADA	SSBN 733
GERALD FORD	CVN 78	TENNESSEE	SSBN 734
		PENNSYLVANIA	SSBN 735
Submarines		WEST VIRGINIA	SSBN 736
		KENTUCKY	SSBN 737
SEAWOLF	SSN 21	MARYLAND	SSBN 738
CONNECTICUT	SSN 22	NEBRASKA	SSBN 739
JIMMY CARTER	SSN 23	RHODE ISLAND	SSBN 740
MEMPHIS	SSN 691	MAINE	SSBN 741
BREMERTON	SSN 698	WYOMING	SSBN 742
JACKSONVILLE	SSN 699	LOUISIANA	SSBN 743
DALLAS	SSN 700	NEWPORT NEWS	SSN 750
LA JOLLA	SSN 701	SAN JUAN	SSN 751
CITY OF CORPUS CHRISTI	SSN 705	PASADENA	SSN 752
ALBUQUERQUE	SSN 706	ALBANY	SSN 753
SAN FRANCISCO	SSN 711	TOPEKA	SSN 754
HOUSTON	SSN 713	MIAMI	SSN 755
NORFOLK	SSN 714	SCRANTON	SSN 756
BUFFALO	SSN 715	ALEXANDRIA	SSN 757
OLYMPIA	SSN 717	ASHEVILLE	SSN 758
PROVIDENCE	SSN 719	JEFFERSON CITY	SSN 759
PITTSBURGH	SSN 720	ANNAPOLIS	SSN 760

Ship	Pennant Number	Ship	Pennant Number
SPRINGFIELD	SSN 761	SAN JACINTO	CG 56
COLUMBUS	SSN 762	LAKE CHAMPLAIN	CG 57
SANTA FE	SSN 763	PHILIPPINE SEA	CG 58
BOISE	SSN 764	PRINCETON	CG 59
MONTPELIER	SSN 765	NORMANDY	CG 60
CHARLOTTE	SSN 766	MONTEREY	CG 61
HAMPTON	SSN 767	CHANCELLORSVILLE	CG 62
HARTFORD	SSN 768	COWPENS	CG 63
TOLEDO	SSN 769	GETTYSBURG	CG 64
TUCSON	SSN 770	CHOSIN	CG 65
COLUMBIA	SSN 771	HUE CITY	CG 66
GREENEVILLE	SSN 772	SHILOH	CG 67
CHEYENNE	SSN 773	ANZIO	CG 68
VIRGINIA	SSN 774	VICKSBURG	CG 69
TEXAS	SSN 775	LAKE ERIE	CG 70
HAWAII	SSN 776	CAPE ST. GEORGE	CG 71
NORTH CAROLINA	SSN 777	VELLA GULF	CG 72
NEW HAMPSHIRE	SSN 778	PORT ROYAL	CG 73
NEW MEXICO	SSN 779		
MISSOURI	SSN 780	**Destroyers**	
CALIFORNIA	SSN 781		
MISSISSIPPI	SSN 782	ARLEIGH BURKE	DDG 51
MINNESOTA	SSN 783	BARRY	DDG 52
NORTH DAKOTA	SSN 784	JOHN PAUL JONES	DDG 53
JOHN WARNER	SSN 785	CURTIS WILBUR	DDG 54
NOT YET NAMED	SSN 786	STOUT	DDG 55
NOT YET NAMED	SSN 787	JOHN S. McCAIN	DDG 56
NOT YET NAMED	SSN 788	MITSCHER	DDG 57
NOT YET NAMED	SSN 789	LABOON	DDG 58
NOT YET NAMED	SSN 790	RUSSELL	DDG 59
NOT YET NAMED	SSN 791	PAUL HAMILTON	DDG 60
		RAMAGE	DDG 61
Cruisers		FITZGERALD	DDG 62
		STETHEM	DDG 63
BUNKER HILL	CG 52	CARNEY	DDG 64
MOBILE BAY	CG 53	BENFOLD	DDG 65
ANTIETAM	CG 54	GONZALEZ	DDG 66
LEYTE GULF	CG 55	COLE	DDG 67

Ship	Pennant Number	Ship	Pennant Number
THE SULLIVANS	DDG 68	STOCKDALE	DDG 106
MILIUS	DDG 69	GRAVELY	DDG 107
HOPPER	DDG 70	WAYNE E. MEYER	DDG 108
ROSS	DDG 71	JASON DUNHAM	DDG 109
MAHAN	DDG 72	WILLIAM P. LAWRENCE	DDG 110
DECATUR	DDG 73	SPRUANCE	DDG 111
McFAUL	DDG 74	MICHAEL MURPHY	DDG 112
DONALD COOK	DDG 75	*NOT YET NAMED*	DDG 113
HIGGINS	DDG 76	*NOT YET NAMED*	DDG 114
O'KANE	DDG 77	*NOT YET NAMED*	DDG 115
PORTER	DDG 78	ZUMWALT	DDG1000
OSCAR AUSTIN	DDG 79	MICHAEL MONSOOR	DDG1001
ROOSEVELT	DDG 80		
WINSTON S. CHURCHILL	DDG 81	**Frigates**	
LASSEN	DDG 82		
HOWARD	DDG 83	BOONE	FFG 28
BULKELEY	DDG 84	STEPHEN W. GROVES	FFG 29
McCAMPBELL	DDG 85	JOHN L. HALL	FFG 32
SHOUP	DDG 86	JARRETT	FFG 33
MASON	DDG 87	UNDERWOOD	FFG 36
PREBLE	DDG 88	CROMMELIN	FFG 37
MUSTIN	DDG 89	CURTS	FFG 38
CHAFEE	DDG 90	DOYLE	FFG 39
PINCKNEY	DDG 91	HALYBURTON	FFG 40
MOMSEN	DDG 92	McCLUSKY	FFG 41
CHUNG-HOON	DDG 93	KLAKRING	FFG 42
NITZE	DDG 94	THACH	FFG 43
JAMES E. WILLIAMS	DDG 95	DE WERT	FFG 45
BAINBRIDGE	DDG 96	RENTZ	FFG 46
HALSEY	DDG 97	NICHOLAS	FFG 47
FORREST SHERMAN	DDG 98	VANDEGRIFT	FFG 48
FARRAGUT	DDG 99	ROBERT G. BRADLEY	FFG 49
KIDD	DDG 100	TAYLOR	FFG 50
GRIDLEY	DDG 101	GARY	FFG 51
SAMPSON	DDG 102	CARR	FFG 52
TRUXTUN	DDG 103	HAWES	FFG 53
STERRETT	DDG 104	FORD	FFG 54
DEWEY	DDG 105	ELROD	FFG 55

Ship	Pennant Number	Ship	Pennant Number
SIMPSON	FFG 56	ANCHORAGE	LPD 23
REUBEN JAMES	FFG 57	ARLINGTON	LPD 24
SAMUEL B. ROBERTS	FFG 58	SOMERSET	LPD 25
KAUFFMAN	FFG 59	WHIDBEY ISLAND	LSD 41
RODNEY M. DAVIS	FFG 60	GERMANTOWN	LSD 42
INGRAHAM	FFG 61	FORT McHENRY	LSD 43
		GUNSTON HALL	LSD 44
Littoral Combat Ships		COMSTOCK	LSD 45
		TORTUGA	LSD 46
FREEDOM	LCS 1	RUSHMORE	LSD 47
INDEPENDENCE	LCS 2	ASHLAND	LSD 48
FORT WORTH	LCS 3	HARPERS FERRY	LSD 49
CORONADO	LCS 4	CARTER HALL	LSD 50
		OAK HILL	LSD 51
Amphibious Ships		PEARL HARBOR	LSD 52
BLUE RIDGE	LCC 19	**Mine Countermeasures Vessels**	
MOUNT WHITNEY	LCC 20		
NASSAU	LHA 4	AVENGER	MCM 1
PELELIU	LHA 5	DEFENDER	MCM 2
AMERICA	LHA 6	SENTRY	MCM 3
WASP	LHD 1	CHAMPION	MCM 4
ESSEX	LHD 2	GUARDIAN	MCM 5
KEARSARGE	LHD 3	DEVASTATOR	MCM 6
BOXER	LHD 4	PATRIOT	MCM 7
BATAAN	LHD 5	SCOUT	MCM 8
BONHOMME RICHARD	LHD 6	PIONEER	MCM 9
IWO JIMA	LHD 7	WARRIOR	MCM 10
MAKIN ISLAND	LHD 8	GLADIATOR	MCM 11
CLEVELAND	LPD 7	ARDENT	MCM 12
DUBUQUE	LPD 8	DEXTROUS	MCM 13
DENVER	LPD 9	CHIEF	MCM 14
PONCE	LPD 15		
SAN ANTONIO	LPD 17	**Patrol Craft**	
NEW ORLEANS	LPD 18		
MESA VERDE	LPD 19	TEMPEST	PC 2
GREEN BAY	LPD 20	HURRICANE	PC 3
NEW YORK	LPD 21	MONSOON	PC 4
SAN DIEGO	LPD 22	TYPHOON	PC 5

Ship	Pennant Number	Ship	Pennant Number
SIROCCO	PC 6	**High Speed Vessel**	
SQUALL	PC 7		
CHINOOK	PC 9	SWIFT	HSV 2
FIREBOLT	PC 10		
WHIRLWIND	PC 11	**Miscellaneous Vessels**	
THUNDERBOLT	PC 12		
		SEA FIGHTER	FSF 1
Joint High Speed Vessel			
		Submarine Tenders	
SPEARHEAD	JHSV 1		
VIGILANT	JHSV 2	EMORY S. LAND	AS 39
FORTITUDE	JHSV 3	FRANK CABLE	AS 40
FALL RIVER	JHSV 4		

USS Maryland

OHIO CLASS SSBN

Ship	Pennant Number	Completion Date	Builder
HENRY M. JACKSON	730	1984	GD (Electric Boat Div)
ALABAMA	731	1985	GD (Electric Boat Div)
ALASKA	732	1986	GD (Electric Boat Div)
NEVADA	733	1986	GD (Electric Boat Div)
TENNESSEE	734	1988	GD (Electric Boat Div)
PENNSYLVANIA	735	1989	GD (Electric Boat Div)
WEST VIRGINIA	736	1990	GD (Electric Boat Div)
KENTUCKY	737	1991	GD (Electric Boat Div)
MARYLAND	738	1992	GD (Electric Boat Div)
NEBRASKA	739	1993	GD (Electric Boat Div)
RHODE ISLAND	740	1994	GD (Electric Boat Div)
MAINE	741	1995	GD (Electric Boat Div)
WYOMING	742	1996	GD (Electric Boat Div)
LOUISIANA	743	1997	GD (Electric Boat Div)

Machinery One nuclear reactor, one shaft **Displacement** 18,750 tons (dived) **Dimensions** 170.7m x 12.8m x 11.1m **Speed** 25 + dived **Armament** 24 - Trident 2 (D5) missiles, 4 Torpedo Tubes **Complement** 155

Notes
These submarines maintain the sea-based leg of the US Nuclear Deterrent Forces, with normally five submarines on station at any one time, five in transit - but still capable of launching missiles - with the remainder in port or overhaul.

All have now been converted to carry the Trident II/D5 missile, the last USS ALABAMA completing modernisation in February 2009.

The 14 Ohio class submarines are undergoing a programme of Engineered Refueling Overhauls (ERO), which refuel the nuclear reactor and overhaul all major systems, allowing the submarines to operate for a further 20 years. The final SSBN ERO will commence in 2018. An analysis of alternatives for the replacement of the Ohio class conducted in 2009 and is currently under review.

The Trident II/D5 is the sixth generation of the Navy's Fleet Ballistic Missile programme, which started in 1955. The D5 is a three-stage, solid propellant, inertial-guided submarine-launched ballistic missile (SLBM) with a range greater than 4,000 nautical miles and accuracy measured in hundreds of feet. The missiles are capable of carrying W76 or W88 Multiple Independently Targeted Re-entry Vehicles (MIRVs). In operation, Trident II/D5 missiles have been declared at eight MIRV warheads under the Strategic Arms Reduction Treaty. In 2007 funding was dedicated to the D5 life extension programme. Full missile procurement began in 2008 and is scheduled to complete in 2012 with a total acquisition of 108 additional missiles.

Two older Lafayette class SSBNs, DANIEL WEBSTER and SAM RAYBURN remain at Charleston as training vessels for nuclear power systems, though their missile compartments have been removed.

Notes on Decommissioning

By law US nuclear-powered vessels must have crews onboard until their reactors have been defuelled. Therefore, when USN submarines are withdrawn from service they are placed "In Commission, In Reserve." Once defuelled and de-equipped they can be decommissioned and removed (stricken) from the Navy Register. Vessels "In Commission, In Reserve" cannot be recalled to active duty.

USS Georgia

OHIO CLASS SSGN

Ship	Pennant Number	Completion Date	Builder
OHIO	726	1981	GD (Electric Boat Div)
MICHIGAN	727	1982	GD (Electric Boat Div)
FLORIDA	728	1983	GD (Electric Boat Div)
GEORGIA	729	1984	GD (Electric Boat Div)

Machinery One nuclear reactor, one shaft **Displacement** 18,750 tons (dived) **Dimensions** 170.7m x 12.8m x 11.1m **Speed** 20 + dived **Armament** Up to 154 Tomahawk missiles, 4 Torpedo Tubes **Complement** 169

Notes

These former Trident submarines were scheduled to be withdrawn from service in 2003/04, however it was decided to convert them to a land attack role. Armed with the Tomahawk missile system, they are also able to carry and support a team of 66 special forces personnel for up to 90 days and insert and retrieve them clandestinely.
OHIO commenced her conversion in November 2003, rejoining the fleet in December 2005. GEORGIA was the last of the four to undergo conversion, completing in March 2008.

14

● GENERAL DYNAMICS ELECTRIC BOAT

USS Missouri

ATTACK SUBMARINES
VIRGINIA CLASS

Ship	Pennant Number	Completion Date	Builder
VIRGINIA	774	2004	GD (Electric Boat Div)
TEXAS	775	2006	Northrop Grumman SB
HAWAII	776	2007	GD (Electric Boat Div)
NORTH CAROLINA	777	2008	Northrop Grumman SB
NEW HAMPSHIRE	778	2008	GD (Electric Boat Div)
NEW MEXICO	779	2010	Northrop Grumman SB
MISSOURI	780	2010	GD (Electric Boat Div)
CALIFORNIA	781	2013	Northrop Grumman SB
MISSISSIPPI	782	2013	GD (Electric Boat Div)
MINNESOTA	783	2014	Northrop Grumman SB
NORTH DAKOTA	784	2014	Northrop Grumman SB
JOHN WARNER	785	2015	GD (Electric Boat Div)

Machinery One nuclear reactor, one shaft **Displacement** 7,800 tons dived **Dimensions** 114.8m x 10.4m x 8m **Speed** 25 knots + dived **Armament** Tomahawk missiles, 12 VLS tubes, Mk48 ADCAP torpedoes, 4 Torpedo Tubes **Complement** 134.

Notes

These advanced submarines are fully configured to conduct mining and mine reconnaissance, Special Operations Forces insertion/extraction, battle group support, intelligence-collection and surveillance missions, sea-control and land attack. Furthermore, the Virginia SSNs will be specifically configured to adapt easily to special missions and emerging requirements.

The first seven submarines, of an anticipated class of 30, are being built under an innovative teaming arrangement between General Dynamics' Electric Boat Corporation (EB) and Northrop Grumman Newport News (NGNN). Under the teaming arrangement, construction of the ships will be shared by ship section. NGNN is building the bow, stern, sail, and selected forward sections for each submarine. EB is building the hull sections, the engine room modules, and the command-and-control system operating spaces. In December 2008, the Navy signed a $14 billion contract with General Dynamics and Northrop Grumman to supply eight submarines (SSN 784 - SSN 791). The contractors delivered one submarine in each of fiscal year 2009 and 2010, and will deliver two submarines in each of fiscal year 2011, 2012 and 2013. This contract will bring the Navy's Virginia class fleet to 18 submarines of a proposed class of 30.

On 21 June 2008, the Navy christened NEW HAMPSHIRE (SSN-778), the first Block II submarine. This boat was delivered eight months ahead of schedule and $54 million under budget. Block II boats are built in four sections, compared to the ten sections of the Block I boats. This enables a cost saving of about $300 million per boat, reducing the overall cost to $2 billion per boat and the construction of two new boats per year.

The single S9G Pressurised Water Reactor is expected to run for 30 years without refuelling. Reportedly as quiet at 25 knots as a Los Angeles class boat at rest.

USS Connecticut

SEAWOLF CLASS

Ship	Pennant Number	Completion Date	Builder
SEAWOLF	21	1997	GD (Electric Boat Div)
CONNECTICUT	22	1998	GD (Electric Boat Div)
JIMMY CARTER	23	2005	GD (Electric Boat Div)

Machinery One nuclear reactor, one shaft **Displacement** 9,284 tons (SSN23 12,353 tons) **Dimensions** 108m x 12m x 11m (SSN23 138.07m x 12.2m) **Speed** 25+ knots **Armament** Tomahawk missiles, Mk48 Torpedoes, 8 torpedo tubes **Complement** 134.

Notes

The US Navy began construction of the Seawolf class in 1989. SSN 23 is roughly 100 feet longer than the rest of the class, being modified during build for highly classified intelligence gathering missions. The extra length is due to the insertion of an additional section known as the Multi-Mission Platform (MMP), which allows launch and recovery of ROVs and Navy SEAL forces. She also has additional maneuvering devices fitted fore and aft that will allow her to keep station over selected targets in any current.

USS Albuquerque

LOS ANGELES CLASS

Ship	Pennant Number	Completion Date	Builder
MEMPHIS	691	1977	Newport News SB
BREMERTON	698	1981	GD (Electric Boat Div)
JACKSONVILLE	699	1981	GD (Electric Boat Div)
DALLAS	700	1981	GD (Electric Boat Div)
LA JOLLA	701	1981	GD (Electric Boat Div)
CITY OF CORPUS CHRISTI	705	1983	GD (Electric Boat Div)
ALBUQUERQUE	706	1983	GD (Electric Boat Div)
SAN FRANCISCO	711	1981	Newport News SB
HOUSTON	713	1982	Newport News SB
NORFOLK	714	1983	Newport News SB
BUFFALO	715	1983	Newport News SB
OLYMPIA	717	1984	Newport News SB
PROVIDENCE	719	1985	GD (Electric Boat Div)
PITTSBURGH	720	1985	GD (Electric Boat Div)

Ship	Pennant Number	Completion Date	Builder
CHICAGO	721	1986	Newport News SB
KEY WEST	722	1987	Newport News SB
OKLAHOMA CITY	723	1988	Newport News SB
LOUISVILLE	724	1986	GD (Electric Boat Div)
HELENA	725	1987	GD (Electric Boat Div)
NEWPORT NEWS	750	1989	Newport News SB
SAN JUAN	751	1988	GD (Electric Boat Div)
PASADENA	752	1989	GD (Electric Boat Div)
ALBANY	753	1990	Newport News SB
TOPEKA	754	1989	GD (Electric Boat Div)
MIAMI	755	1990	GD (Electric Boat Div)
SCRANTON	756	1991	Newport News SB
ALEXANDRIA	757	1991	GD (Electric Boat Div)
ASHEVILLE	758	1991	Newport News SB
JEFFERSON CITY	759	1992	Newport News SB
ANNAPOLIS	760	1992	GD (Electric Boat Div)
SPRINGFIELD	761	1993	GD (Electric Boat Div)
COLUMBUS	762	1993	GD (Electric Boat Div)
SANTA FE	7631	1994	GD (Electric Boat Div)
BOISE	764	1992	Newport News SB
MONTPELIER	765	1993	Newport News SB
CHARLOTTE	766	1994	Newport News SB
HAMPTON	767	1993	Newport News SB
HARTFORD	768	1994	GD (Electric Boat Div)
TOLEDO	769	1995	Newport News SB
TUCSON	770	1995	Newport News SB
COLUMBIA	771	1995	GD (Electric Boat Div)
GREENVILLE	772	1996	Newport News SB
CHEYENNE	773	1996	Newport News SB

Machinery One nuclear reactor, one shaft **Displacement** 7,011 tonnes **Dimensions** 110m x 10m x 9.7 **Speed** 20+ knots **Armament** Tomahawk missiles, vertical launch tubes (719 and later) Mk 48 torpedoes, four torpedo tubes **Complement** 140

Notes

Designed as a follow-on to the STURGEON class submarines built during the 1960s, the Los Angeles class incorporated improved sound quietening and a larger propulsion plant than previous classes. Her many capabilities include wartime functions of undersea warfare, surface warfare, strike warfare, mining operations, special forces delivery, reconnaissance, carrier battle group support and escort, and intelligence collection. This large class of submarine evolved during construction and three variants eventually entered service.

From PROVIDENCE onwards the submarines were fitted with 12 vertical launch tubes for the Tomahawk cruise missile, along with an upgraded reactor core. The final 23 hulls (SAN JUAN and later) are referred to as the Improved Los Angeles (or 688I Class). These submarines are quieter, incorporating an advanced BSY-1 sonar suite and the ability to lay mines from their torpedo tubes. Their forward diving planes were moved from the conning tower (sail) to the bow and the sail has been strengthened for breaking through ice.

In 2005 SAN FRANCISCO collided with a seamount causing extensive damage. Following a survey it was determined that she should be repaired and her forward section was replaced with that from the decommissioned HONOLULU. The $79 million repair was completed in October 2008 and SAN FRANCISCO returned to the fleet.

Following a collision with USS NEW ORLEANS in the Gulf in 2009, which caused extensive structural damage to her sail, HARTFORD was returned to the fleet in 2010 on completion of repairs.

USS LOS ANGELES decommissioned in January 2010; PHILADELPHIA in June 2010. MEMPHIS is scheduled to decommission in March 2011.

Submarine Rescue

The Submarine Rescue Diving and Recompression System's (SRDRS) Rescue Capable System (RCS) replaced the Deep Submergence Rescue Vehicle MYSTIC (DSRV-1) as the US Navy's deep-submergence submarine rescue asset on 30 September 2008. MYSTIC and the DSRV programme began deactivation the following month.

SRDRS is a rapidly deployable rescue asset that can be delivered by air or ground, installed on pre-screened military or commercial vessels of opportunity (VOO) via a ship interface template, and mated to a distressed submarine within a 72-hour time to first rescue period.

For the past 30 years, MYSTIC, one of a pair of small rescue submarines capable of deploying via air or ground, had to be delivered to a port where it was mated to a specially-configured submarine which served as the host platform for the voyage to the disabled submarine.

The replacement SRDRS is a three-phased acquisition programme that will deliver advanced submarine rescue and treatment assets to the fleet. The first phase was the Atmospheric Dive System 2000 (ADS2000) which was delivered to the Navy in 2006. ADS2000 is a manned, one-atmosphere dive suit capable of inspecting disabled submarines and clearing debris from escape hatches. The RCS constitutes SRDRS' second phase.

SRDRS-RCS consists of FALCON, a tethered, remotely-operated Pressurized Rescue Module (PRM), its launch and recovery system, and its support equipment; all of which are controlled from a VOO.

The final phase of the SRDRS programme is the Submarine Decompression System (SDS), scheduled for delivery in late 2012. SDS will allow rescued submariners to remain under pressure during the transfer from the PRM to hyperbaric treatment chambers aboard the VOO.

Unlike MYSTIC, which could only be transported to the disabled submarine via modified submarines, SRDRS is a "fly-away" system that can quickly and easily be mobilised via large military or civilian transport aircraft and installed aboard a variety of VOOs within hours of notification of a submarine in distress.

FALCON can conduct rescue operations to a depth of 2,000 feet, can mate to a disabled submarine at a list and trim of up to 45 degrees, and can transfer up to 16 personnel at a time. Because SRDRS-RCS receives its power from a VOO via an umbilical, it can operate around the clock without pause.

SRDRS underwent a test and operational evaluation during the international submarine rescue exercise Bold Monarch in May-June 2008, during which SRDRS demonstrated its ability to mate and transfer personnel from three participating submarines. More recently, it has demonstrated its capabilities during an exercise with the Chilean submarine CS SIMPSON.

SRDRS is based at San Diego, and operated by the Navy's Deep Submergence Unit.

USS Gerald Ford

GERALD FORD CLASS

Ship	Pennant Number	Completion Date	Builder
GERALD FORD	CVN 78	*Building*	Newport News SB

Machinery Two nuclear reactors driving four shafts **Displacement** 100,000 tons full load **Dimensions** 333m x 41m (Flight Deck width 78m) x 12.4m **Speed** 30+ knots **Armament** Two Sea Sparrow missile launchers, three Phalanx 20 mm CIWS mounts, two RIM-116 RAM launchers **Aircraft** 75+ **Complement** 4,660 (including aircrew).

Notes

Contract awarded for the detailed design, long lead procurement and advanced construction in May 2004. GERALD FORD is scheduled for delivery in 2015 with two further ships, CVN 79 and CVN 80, scheduled to enter service in 2020 and 2025. The CVN 21 class will incorporate such features as: a new, more efficient nuclear propulsion plant, an Electro-Magnetic Aircraft Launch System (EMALS), Advanced Arresting Gear (AAG), and a nearly three-fold increase in electrical generation capacity over that of Nimitz-class carriers. These improvements, coupled with an expanded Flight Deck and other topside changes designed to increase operational efficiency, will provide higher sortie generation rates. At the same time, manpower requirements for the ship and air wing will be significantly reduced.

USS George H. W. Bush

AIRCRAFT CARRIERS
NIMITZ CLASS

Ship	Pennant Number	Completion Date	Builder
NIMITZ	CVN 68	1975	Newport News SB
DWIGHT D. EISENHOWER	CVN 69	1977	Newport News SB
CARL VINSON	CVN 70	1982	Newport News SB
THEODORE ROOSEVELT	CVN 71	1986	Newport News SB
ABRAHAM LINCOLN	CVN 72	1989	Newport News SB
GEORGE WASHINGTON	CVN 73	1992	Newport News SB
JOHN C. STENNIS	CVN 74	1995	Newport News SB
HARRY S. TRUMAN	CVN 75	1998	Newport News SB
RONALD REAGAN	CVN 76	2003	Newport News SB
GEORGE H.W. BUSH	CVN 77	2008	Newport News SB

Machinery Two nuclear reactors driving four shafts **Displacement** 91,487 tons full load (CVN 68-70), 96,386 tons full load (CVN 71), 102,000 tons full load (CVN 72-74) **Dimensions** 332.9m x 40.8m x 11.3m (CVN 68-70) 11.8m (CVN 71) 11.9m (CVN 72-74) **Speed** 30+ knots **Armament** Two or three (depending on modification) NATO Sea Sparrow launchers, 20mm Phalanx CIWS mounts: (3 on CVN 68 and CVN 69, 4 on later ships.) **Aircraft** 85 **Complement** 3,200 plus 2,480 air wing.

Notes
Expected to operate for 15 years between refuellings. The last two of the class have a prominent bow bulb to improve seakeeping and the island structure is one deck lower than on previous ships of the class. Both have larger "one piece" jet blast deflectors and flight deck operations re-orientated to the port side of the ship. A longer angled deck extension makes simultaneous landing and take off operations possible.

GEORGE H W BUSH was delivered in 2008 as the numerical replacement for KITTY HAWK, which then retired after 47 years, the last conventionally powered aircraft carrier in service.

USS Enterprise

ENTERPRISE CLASS

Ship	Pennant Number	Completion Date	Builder
ENTERPRISE	CVN 65	1961	Newport News SB

Machinery Eight nuclear reactors driving four shafts **Displacement** 89,600 tons full load **Dimensions** 335.64m x 39.9m (75.6m flight deck width) x 11.9m **Speed** 30+ knots **Armament** Two Sea Sparrow missile launchers, three Phalanx 20 mm CIWS mounts **Aircraft** 85 **Complement** 3,350 - Air Wing 2,480.

Notes

Almost 50 years old, ENTERPRISE is expected to remain in service until 2015 when she should be replaced by GERALD FORD (CVN 78). She has four rudders (as opposed to two on the Nimitz class) and eight nuclear reactors. Two are kept non-operational, reducing her top speed to 31 knots from her designed speed of 36.

USS Vella Gulf

CRUISERS

TICONDEROGA CLASS

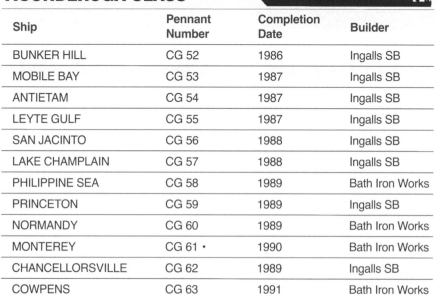

Ship	Pennant Number	Completion Date	Builder
BUNKER HILL	CG 52	1986	Ingalls SB
MOBILE BAY	CG 53	1987	Ingalls SB
ANTIETAM	CG 54	1987	Ingalls SB
LEYTE GULF	CG 55	1987	Ingalls SB
SAN JACINTO	CG 56	1988	Ingalls SB
LAKE CHAMPLAIN	CG 57	1988	Ingalls SB
PHILIPPINE SEA	CG 58	1989	Bath Iron Works
PRINCETON	CG 59	1989	Ingalls SB
NORMANDY	CG 60	1989	Bath Iron Works
MONTEREY	CG 61 •	1990	Bath Iron Works
CHANCELLORSVILLE	CG 62	1989	Ingalls SB
COWPENS	CG 63	1991	Bath Iron Works

Ship	Pennant Number	Completion Date	Builder
GETTYSBURG	CG 64	1991	Bath Iron Works
CHOSIN	CG 65	1991	Ingalls SB
HUE CITY	CG 66	1991	Ingalls SB
SHILOH	CG 67 •	1992	Bath Iron Works
ANZIO	CG 68	1992	Ingalls SB
VICKSBURG	CG 69	1992	Ingalls SB
LAKE ERIE	CG 70 •	1993	Bath Iron Works
CAPE ST GEORGE	CG 71	1993	Ingalls SB
VELLA GULF	CG 72 •	1993	Ingalls SB
PORT ROYAL	CG 73 •	1994	Ingalls SB

Machinery Four GE LM2500 gas turbine engines; Two shafts, 80,000 shp **Displacement** 9,600 tons **Dimensions** 172.8m x 16.8m x 9.5m **Speed** 30+ knots **Armament** Mk 41 VLS Standard Missile (MR); Vertical Launch ASROC Missile; Tomahawk Cruise Missile; Six Mk 46 torpedoes (two triple mounts); Two Mk 45 5-inch/54 calibre guns; Two Phalanx close-in-weapons systems **Aircraft** Two SH-60 Seahawk **Complement** 364

Notes

Cruisers of the USN are general purpose, or Multi-mission ships, designed to operate within a battle group. Capable of conducting anti-air, anti-submarine, anti-surface and long range strike warfare the ships usually support Carrier Strike Groups (CSG) and Expeditionary Strike Groups (ESG). They can also operate independently and as flag-ships of surface action groups. All of the early Mk 26 missile launcher fitted ships have been decommissioned, TICONDEROGA being the first to go in 2004. The remaining ships are expected to serve for at least 35 years and will be subject to the AEGIS Cruiser Modernisation programme which will see improvements in war-fighting capability through enhanced self defence (CIWS Block 1B, Evolved Sea Sparrow Missile (ESSM)), Cooperative Engagement Capability (CEC), improved littoral ASW capability and signif-icant land attack improvements (Tactical Tomahawk - TACTOM). A comprehensive Mission Life Extension (MLE) package will include hull, machinery and electrical system upgrades and a series of alterations designed to restore displacement and stability mar-gins, correct hull and superstructure cracking and improve accommodation spaces.

Five vessels (indicated with • in listing above) are equipped with the Aegis Ballistic Missile Defence System. For full details see page 30. CHOSIN was slated to start its $50 million upgrade in January 2011 through the Cruiser Modernisation programme at Pearl Harbour Naval Shipyard.

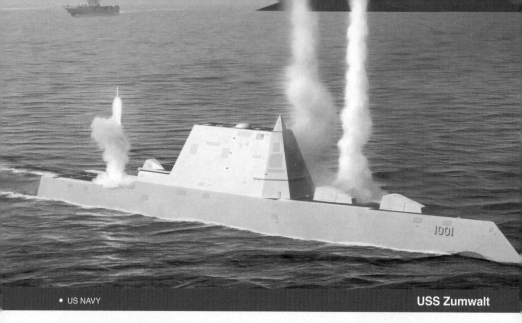

USS Zumwalt

DESTROYERS
ZUMWALT CLASS

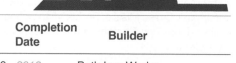

Ship	Pennant Number	Completion Date	Builder
ZUMWALT	DDG 1000	*2013*	Bath Iron Works
MICHAEL MONSOOR	DDG 1001	*2014*	Northrop Grumman

Machinery Integrated Propulsion System; Two Main Turbine Generators; Two Propulsion Motors **Displacement** 14,564 tons full load **Dimensions** 182.3m x 24.6m x 8.4m **Speed** 30 knots **Armament** Vertical Launch System, comprising 80 missiles (Standard SM-2, Evolved Sea Sparrow Missile (ESSM), Tactical Tomahawk, ASROC), 2 x 155 mm Advanced Gun System, 2 x 57mm CIWS **Aircraft** Two helicopters or three UAVs or combination of both **Complement** Approx 140.

Notes

The Zumwalt-class are designed as multi-mission ships with a focus on land attack, though in reality are a cheaper, watered-down version of the proposed DD-21 class. Initially perceived as a class of up to 30 ships, in July 2008 the Navy decided to terminate the expensive programme at just three ships, preferring instead to extend production of the Arleigh Burke class. The vessel has a unique wave-piercing tumblehome hull form and a low radar cross-section with all sensors being mounted within the superstructure.

USS Hopper

ARLEIGH BURKE CLASS
Flight I & Flight II

Ship	Pennant Number	Completion Date	Builder
ARLEIGH BURKE	DDG 51	1991	Bath Iron Works
BARRY	DDG 52	1992	Ingalls SB
JOHN PAUL JONES	DDG 53 •	1993	Bath Iron Works
CURTIS WILBUR	DDG 54 •	1994	Bath Iron Works
STOUT	DDG 55 •	1994	Ingalls SB
JOHN S. McCAIN	DDG 56 •	1994	Bath Iron Works
MITSCHER	DDG 57	1995	Ingalls SB
LABOON	DDG 58	1995	Bath Iron Works

Ship	Pennant Number	Completion Date	Builder
RUSSELL	DDG 59 •	1995	Ingalls SB
PAUL HAMILTON	DDG 60 •	1995	Bath Iron Works
RAMAGE	DDG 61 •	1995	Ingalls SB
FITZGERALD	DDG 62 •	1995	Bath Iron Works
STETHEM	DDG 63 •	1995	Ingalls SB
CARNEY	DDG 64	1996	Bath Iron Works
BENFOLD	DDG 65 •	1996	Ingalls SB
GONZALEZ	DDG 66	1996	Bath Iron Works
COLE	DDG 67	1996	Ingalls SB
THE SULLIVANS	DDG 68	1997	Bath Iron Works
MILIUS	DDG 69 •	1996	Ingalls SB
HOPPER	DDG 70 •	1997	Bath Iron Works
ROSS	DDG 71	1997	Ingalls SB
MAHAN	DDG 72	1998	Bath Iron Works
DECATUR	DDG 73 •	1998	Bath Iron Works
McFAUL	DDG 74	1998	Ingalls SB
DONALD COOK	DDG 75	1998	Bath Iron Works
HIGGINS	DDG 76 •	1999	Bath Iron Works
O'KANE	DDG 77 •	1999	Bath Iron Works
PORTER	DDG 78	1999	Ingalls SB

Machinery Four GE LM2500-30 gas turbines; two shafts; 100,000shp **Displacement** 9,033 tons **Dimensions** 153.92m x 18m x 6.3m **Speed** 30+ knots **Armament** Mk 41 VLS Standard missile; Harpoon; VLS ASROC missiles; Tomahawk; six Mk 46 torpedoes (two triple tube mounts); one 5-inch/54 calibre gun **Aircraft** Landing facilities aft, but no hangar **Complement** 323.

Notes

Just like the cruisers, the modern day USN destroyer is a multi-mission vessel able to operate independently, or as part of a larger group, across all warfare disciplines. The combat system centres around the Aegis combat system and the SPY-1D, multi-function phased array radar. Flight II ships (from DDG 72) incorporate Link 16, SLQ 32(V) EW suite, extended range surface-air missiles and improved tactical information exchange systems. These ships also carry greater reserves of fuel, thus extending their range. The lack of an embarked helicopter on a vessel of this size has been a disadvantage and the follow-on Flight IIA ships have been redesigned to incorporate a hangar and flight deck.

The USN is introducing an Anti-Ballistic Missile programme centring around an upgraded Aegis system coupled with the SM-3 missile, providing the fleet with an ABM tracking and shoot-down capability. The first Block I production SM-3 was delivered in October 2004, and the Aegis 3.0 update was delivered in 2005.

This system was given greater importance by President Obama in September 2009, when plans to scrap a land-based missile defence site in Poland, in favour of a missile system located on US Navy warships was announced. By that time several US Navy ships were fitted with SM-3 missiles to serve this function. Current Aegis BMD hardware includes the SM-3 Block-1a missile and other improvements to the Aegis Weapons System.

A total of five US Navy Ticonderoga class cruisers and 15 Arleigh Burke class destroyers have BMD capability as of 2010. All remaining Ticonderoga class cruisers that have SPY-1B systems (CG-59 - CG-73) are to be refitted with TBMD engagement technology.

Ticonderoga class cruisers equipped with anti-ballistic missile capability include LAKE ERIE, SHILOH and PORT ROYAL. Arleigh Burke class destroyers so equipped include CURTIS WILBUR, STOUT, JOHN S. McCAIN, RUSSELL, PAUL HAMILTON, RAMAGE, FITZGERALD, USS STETHEM, BENFOLD, MILIUS, DECATUR and O'KANE.

An additional three ships have been refitted for Long Range Surveillance and Tracking (LRST): JOHN PAUL JONES, HOPPER and HIGGINS, though it was expected that all three should be upgraded to add engagement capabilities by 2010.

In November 2009, the Missile Defence Agency announced that six additional destroyers would be upgraded to participate in the programme. In 2012, CARNEY, ROSS, and DONALD COOK will be upgraded. COLE, McFAUL and PORTER will be upgraded in 2013. The goal of the programme is to have 21 ships upgraded by the end of 2010; 24 in 2012; 27 around 2013 and 38 at the end of FY 2015.

USS Gravely

ARLEIGH BURKE CLASS
Flight IIA

Ship	Pennant Number	Completion Date	Builder
OSCAR AUSTIN	DDG 79	2000	Bath Iron Works
ROOSEVELT	DDG 80	2000	Ingalls SB
WINSTON S. CHURCHILL	DDG 81	2001	Bath Iron Works
LASSEN	DDG 82	2001	Ingalls SB
HOWARD	DDG 83	2001	Bath Iron Works
BULKELEY	DDG 84	2001	Ingalls SB
McCAMPBELL	DDG 85	2002	Bath Iron Works
SHOUP	DDG 86	2002	Ingalls SB
MASON	DDG 87	2003	Bath Iron Works
PREBLE	DDG 88	2002	Ingalls SB

Ship	Pennant Number	Completion Date	Builder
MUSTIN	DDG 89	2003	Ingalls SB
CHAFEE	DDG 90	2003	Bath Iron Works
PINCKNEY	DDG 91	2004	Ingalls SB
MOMSEN	DDG 92	2004	Bath Iron Works
CHUNG-HOON	DDG 93	2004	Ingalls SB
NITZE	DDG 94	2004	Bath Iron Works
JAMES E. WILLIAMS	DDG 95	2004	Ingalls SB
BAINBRIDGE	DDG 96	2005	Bath Iron Works
HALSEY	DDG 97	2005	Ingalls SB
FORREST SHERMAN	DDG 98	2006	Ingalls SB
FARRAGUT	DDG 99	2006	Bath Iron Works
KIDD	DDG 100	2007	Ingalls SB
GRIDLEY	DDG 101	2007	Bath Iron Works
SAMPSON	DDG 102	2007	Bath Iron Works
TRUXTUN	DDG 103	2009	Ingalls SB
STERETT	DDG 104	2008	Bath Iron Works
DEWEY	DDG 105	2010	Ingalls SB
STOCKDALE	DDG 106	2009	Bath Iron Works
GRAVELY	DDG 107	2010	Ingalls SB
WAYNE E MEYER	DDG 108	2009	Bath Iron Works
JASON DUNHAM	DDG 109	2010	Bath Iron Works
WILLIAM P LAWRENCE	DDG 110	*Building*	Ingalls SB
SPRUANCE	DDG 111	*Building*	Bath Iron Works
MICHAEL MURPHY	DDG 112	*Building*	Bath Iron Works

Machinery Four GE LM 2500-30 gas turbines; two shafts; 100,000shp **Displacement** 9,217 tons **Dimensions** 155.3m x 20.4m x 6.3m **Speed** 30+ knots **Armament** Mk 41 VLS Standard missile; VLS ASROC missiles; Tomahawk; six Mk 46 torpedoes (two triple tube mounts); one 5-inch/54 calibre gun **Aircraft** Two SH-60 Seahawk helicopters **Complement** 323

Notes

The Flight IIA ships incorporate facilities to support two embarked helicopters, significantly enhancing the ship's sea-control capabilities. These ships have the Aegis combat system Baseline 6 Phase 3, which incorporates Cooperative Engagement Capability (CEC) and the Evolved Sea Sparrow Missile (ESSM). The Harpoon canisters have been removed as a weight saving measure, but could be re-installed, if needed, between the funnels. They have six extra VLS cells. The improved SPY- 1D(V) radar, the Remote Mine-Hunting System (RMS), as well as advanced open architecture combat systems using commercially developed processors and display equipment were introduced as part of Baseline 7 Phase 1, commencing with DDG-91. The DDG-51 programme was planned to stop at 62 ships (DDG-112 being the 62nd) but, in July 2008, the Navy announced plans to truncate the DDG-1000 programme at three ships and reopen the DDG-51 line to better align surface combatant investment strategy. It was intended to restart the DDG-51 line with one ship in 2010, two in 2011, one in 2012, two in 2013 and one each in 2014 and 2015. The keel for MICHAEL MURPHY was laid down on 18 June 2010 at Bath Iron Works.

Additionally, in 2008 the Senate Armed Services Committee viewed the plan to operate the DDG-51 class for a full 40 years to be very high risk and directed the Secretary of the Navy to submit a modernisation acquisition strategy report to the congressional defence committees with the fiscal year 2010 budget request. The report was to include a plan to execute a pilot project that would accomplish the full scope of DDG-51 hull, mechanical and electrical, and combat system maintenance and modernisation during a single refit period.

The completion of TRUXTUN was delayed having suffered a major electrical fire during construction on 20 May 2006 engulfing two levels and causing damage in the millions of dollars.

     USS Taylor

FRIGATES
OLIVER HAZARD PERRY CLASS

Ship	Pennant Number	Completion Date	Builder
BOONE	FFG 28	1982	Todd SY, Seattle
STEPHEN W. GROVES	FFG 29	1982	Bath Iron Works
JOHN L. HALL	FFG 32	1982	Bath Iron Works
JARRETT	FFG 33	1983	Todd SY, San Pedro
UNDERWOOD	FFG 36	1983	Bath Iron Works
CROMMELIN	FFG 37	1983	Todd SY, Seattle
CURTS	FFG 38	1983	Todd SY, San Pedro
DOYLE	FFG 39	1983	Bath Iron Works
HALYBURTON	FFG 40	1984	Todd SY, Seattle
McCLUSKEY	FFG 41	1983	Todd SY, San Pedro
KLAKRING	FFG 42	1983	Bath Iron Works
THACH	FFG 43	1984	Todd SY, San Pedro
DE WERT	FFG 45	1983	Bath Iron Works

Ship	Pennant Number	Completion Date	Builder
RENTZ	FFG 46	1984	Todd SY, San Pedro
NICHOLAS	FFG 47	1984	Bath Iron Works
VANDEGRIFT	FFG 48	1984	Todd SY, Seattle
ROBERT G. BRADLEY	FFG 49	1984	Bath Iron Works
TAYLOR	FFG 50	1984	Bath Iron Works
GARY	FFG 51	1984	Todd SY, San Pedro
CARR	FFG 52	1985	Todd SY, Seattle
HAWES	FFG 53	1985	Bath Iron Works
FORD	FFG 54	1985	Todd SY, San Pedro
ELROD	FFG 55	1985	Bath Iron Works
SIMPSON	FFG 56	1985	Bath Iron Works
REUBEN JAMES	FFG 57	1986	Todd SY, San Pedro
SAMUEL B. ROBERTS	FFG 58	1986	Bath Iron Works
KAUFMANN	FFG 59	1987	Bath Iron Works
RODNEY M. DAVIS	FFG 60	1987	Todd SY, San Pedro
INGRAHAM	FFG 61	1989	Todd SY, San Pedro

Machinery Two GE LM2500 gas turbine engines; 1 shaft; 41,000shp **Displacement** 4,100 tonnes **Dimensions** 135.6m x 13.7m x 4.5m **Speed** 29 knots **Armament** Six Mk 46 torpedoes (two triple mounts); One 76 mm (3-inch)/62 calibre Mk 75 rapid fire gun; One Phalanx close-in-weapons system **Aircraft** Two SH-60 Seahawk **Complement** 215

Notes

Originally a class of 51 vessels, these low cost single screw frigates were designed as cost efficient surface combatants, however they lack the multi-mission capability necessary for modern surface combatants faced with multiple, high-technology threats. They also offer limited capacity for growth. They were fitted with a single Mk 13 missile launcher forward of the bridge for Harpoon and Standard missiles, but this has since been removed and in some cases replaced by a 25mm gun mounted on a frame above the old launcher. Their primary role today is anti-submarine protection of amphibious groups, auxiliaries and merchant shipping.

McINERNEY was transferred to Pakistan in 2010 and renamed PNS ALAMGIR. HAWES is scheduled to decommission by the end of 2010 and be used as a source of spares. JARRETT and DOYLE are to be set aside for foreign sale in 2011.

USS Freedom

LITTORAL COMBAT SHIPS
FREEDOM CLASS

Ship	Pennant Number	Completion Date	Builder
FREEDOM	LCS 1	2008	LM/Marinette Marine Shipyard
FORT WORTH	LCS 3	*2012*	LM/Marinette Marine Shipyard

Machinery Combined diesel and gas turbine with steerable water jet propulsion **Displacement** 3,000 tonnes **Dimensions** 115m x 13m x 4m **Speed** 45+ knots **Armament** One Bofors 57mm; one RAM launcher; four .50 calibre MG; additional weapons can be added depending on role **Complement** 15 core crew (up to 75 max.)

Notes

One of two designs being constructed under a 2006 contract . The contract for the Flight 0 vessels is for two vessels of each design, with an ultimate requirement for up to 60 vessels. The Lockheed Martin design is for a semi-planing steel mono-hull. The vessels weapons and sensor packages will be of a modular design, allowing the vessels to be re-roled within a very short space of time (as quickly as 24 hours in some cases). They can be equipped for anti-surface, anti-submarine, mine warfare or surveillance duties. FREEDOM will be manned by one of two rotational crews, blue and gold, similar to the rotational crews assigned to Trident submarines. The crews can be augmented by one of three mission package crews during focused mission assignments. All vessels are to bear the names of small and medium sized US cities. The first four vessels are to be based at San Diego.

INDEPENDENCE CLASS

Ship	Pennant Number	Completion Date	Builder
INDEPENDENCE	LCS 2	2009	GD/ Austal USA
CORONADO	LCS 4	*2012*	GD/ Austal USA

Machinery Combined diesel and Gas Turbines with steerable waterjet propulsion **Displacement** 2,880 tonnes **Dimensions** 127.1m x 30.4m x 4.5m **Speed** 45 knots **Armament** One Bofors 57mm; one RAM launcher; four .50 calibre MG; additional weapons can be added depending on role **Complement** 50 core crew (up to 75)

Notes

An aluminium trimaran design from Austal/General Dynamics, offering a large flight deck and helicopter handling capability on a relatively small displacement vessel, the hangar being able to accommodate two Seahawk helicopters, while the flight deck can handle helicopters the size of the CH-53 Sea Stallion.

As we went to press in late 2010 a decision was expected on which of the two competing designs would be selected for full scale production.

USS Patriot

MINE COUNTERMEASURES SHIPS
AVENGER CLASS

Ship	Pennant Number	Completion Date	Builder
AVENGER	MCM 1	1987	Peterson Builders Inc.
DEFENDER	MCM 2	1989	Marinette Marine Corp.
SENTRY	MCM 3	1989	Peterson Builders Inc.
CHAMPION	MCM 4	1991	Marinette Marine Corp.
GUARDIAN	MCM 5	1989	Peterson Builders Inc.
DEVASTATOR	MCM 6	1990	Peterson Builders Inc.
PATRIOT	MCM 7	1991	Marinette Marine Corp.
SCOUT	MCM 8	1990	Peterson Builders Inc.
PIONEER	MCM 9	1992	Peterson Builders Inc.
WARRIOR	MCM 10	1993	Peterson Builders Inc.
GLADIATOR	MCM 11	1993	Peterson Builders Inc.
ARDENT	MCM 12	1994	Peterson Builders Inc.
DEXTROUS	MCM 13	1994	Peterson Builders Inc.
CHIEF	MCM 14	1994	Peterson Builders Inc.

Machinery Four diesels (each 600shp); two shafts with controllable pitch propellers **Displacement** 1,450 tons **Dimensions** 68.4m x 11.9m x 3.7m **Speed** 13.5 knots **Armament** 2 x 12.7 MG (MCM11 1 x 25mm 88 Bushmaster; 1 x 7.63 Gatling MG) **Complement** 84.

Notes

Designed as minehunter-killers capable of finding, classifying and destroying moored and bottom mines. They retain a conventional minesweeping capability. Can deploy and operate independently. The hulls of the ships are constructed of oak, Douglas Fir and Alaskan Cedar, with a thin coating of fibreglass to take advantage of woods low magnetic signature during mine countermeasures operations.

The class has been undergoing a modernisation programme since 2004 aimed at correcting maintenance and obsolescence issues. The MCM-1 modernization package includes Planned Product Improvement Programme (PPIP) on the Isotta Fraschini main engines and generators for MCM-3 through MCM-14; replacement of the obsolete Mine Neutralisation Vehicle with a commercial Expendable Mine Neutralisation System (EMNS); and upgrading the existing SQQ-32 Sonar with High Frequency Wide Band capabilities. Other major HM&E alterations include 400-Hz modifications, replacement of Aft Deck hydraulic equipment with electric equipment, replacement of the diesel generator analogue voltage regulators with digital voltage regulators, and upgrading the common navigation system.

In 2009 the MCM fleet relocated following the closure of Naval Station Ingleside, Texas. All are now home ported at San Diego. PATRIOT and GUARDIAN are forward deployed to Sasebo, Japan while ARDENT, DEXTEROUS, GLADIATOR and SCOUT are forward deployed to Bahrain.

USS Tempest & Monsoon

PATROL SHIPS (COASTAL)
CYCLONE CLASS

Ship	Pennant Number	Completion Date	Builder
TEMPEST	PC 2	1993	Bollinger, Lockport
HURRICANE	PC 3	1993	Bollinger, Lockport
MONSOON	PC 4	1994	Bollinger, Lockport
TYPHOON	PC 5	1994	Bollinger, Lockport
SIROCCO	PC 6	1994	Bollinger, Lockport
SQUALL	PC 7	1994	Bollinger, Lockport
CHINOOK	PC 9	1995	Bollinger, Lockport
FIREBOLT	PC 10	1995	Bollinger, Lockport
WHIRLWIND	PC 11	1995	Bollinger, Lockport
THUNDERBOLT	PC 12	1995	Bollinger, Lockport

Machinery Four Paxman diesels; four shafts; 3,350 shp **Displacement** 336 tonnes **Dimensions** 51.8m x 7.6m x 2.4m **Speed** 35 knots **Armament** One Mk 96 and one Mk 38 25mm MG; Five .50 calibre MG; two Mk 19 40mm automatic grenade launchers; Two M-60 machine guns **Complement** 28

Notes

At one time this was a class of ship looking for a role within the "blue water" US Navy. Now, with a shift of emphasis to littoral operations, these coastal patrol craft have become key players in the patrol, interdiction and surveillance roles in a shallow water environment. Six vessels are stationed at NAB Little Creek on the Atlantic coast and two at NAB Coronado, on the Pacific coast, though it is frequent now for up to five to be forward deployed to Bahrain. On 30 September 2004 TEMPEST (PC 2), MONSOON, (PC 4), ZEPHYR, (PC 8), SHAMAL, (PC 13) and TORNADA, (PC 14) were decommissioned and transferred to the US Coast Guard, on loan for four years. TEMPEST and MONSOON were returned to the USN in August 2008, the remainder are scheduled to follow in 2011. The Navy retain ownership of the vessels and are responsible for maintenance. CYCLONE (PC 1) was transferred to the Philippine Navy in 2003.

Beginning in 2009, the ships are undergoing a sustainment programme to update the ships communication, engineering and support systems. Several vessels sport modified bows with a raised bulwark at deck level.

In September 2010 vessels homeported in Bahrain and Norfolk revealed significant structural damage. As a result the Navy decided to cease operations of the vessels in the Persian Gulf until they could be permanently repaired and restored to designed capability. All five ships in the 5th Fleet Area of Operations (PCs 5, 6, 9, 10, 11) have been inspected. All vessels have experienced frame buckling and damage to the hull. Corrosion is also evident.

Detailed inspections of the PCs based in Norfolk (PCs 2, 3, 4, 7, 12) were underway in late 2010. A plan to expeditiously complete any necessary repairs on those vessels will be developed based on the results of the completed inspections. Those vessels remaining in operation during the inspections will be used to maintain crew proficiency and will be subject to sea state and speed restrictions until repairs are completed. The Navy was also coordinating with the US Coast Guard to begin inspections on the three vessels (PCs 8, 13, 14) currently on loan from the Navy.

38-foot Riverine Patrol Craft of RIVRON1

RIVERINE UNITS

The Riverine Squadrons were re-established in 2006 as elements of the Navy Expeditionary Combat Command (NECC). Their task is to conduct Maritime Security Operations and Theatre Security Cooperation in a riverine area of operations or other suitable area. The force is capable of combating enemy riverine forces by direct or supporting fire.

By 2008 there were three Riverine Squadrons in service all operating under the command of Riverine Group One (RIVGRU1) located at Norfolk. Squadrons One and Two are based at Norfolk and Squadron Three at Yorktown. A fourth squadron focused on Security Force Assistance training and manned within the reserve component was funded in FY 2011.

Initially some 1980s vintage, aluminium hulled, 35-foot Riverine Assault Craft were brought forward from reserve, armed with .50-calibre guns at the front and rear. These have since been replaced by 38-foot vessels that are quieter, have an open bow that holds more cargo and troops, a front ramp and bigger diesel engines. The squadrons primarily use three types of boat; the Riverine Command Boat; Riverine Patrol Boat and the Riverine Assault Boat.

Since being re-established the squadrons have regularly deployed to Iraq on security and patrol operations.

Sea Ark

INSHORE BOAT UNITS

Coastal and harbour defence and protection of naval assets are placed under the jurisdiction of two Naval Coastal Warfare Groups: one for the Pacific Fleet and one for the Atlantic Fleet. Within these groups are Mobile Security Squadrons and Naval Coastal Warfare Squadrons. MSSs deploy Mobile Security Detachments that provide force protection for high value naval targets in ports and harbours where US shore infrastructure is limited or does not exist. Naval Coastal Warfare Squadrons provide surveillance and security in harbours, coasts, and inshore areas. They comprise Mobile Inshore Undersea Warfare Units (MIUWUs) and Inshore Boat Units (IBUs). MIUWUs are charged with security, observation, and communications support for commanders operating in an inshore/coast environment, including anchorages and harbours. In the same operating environment, IBUs manage water craft for security, interdiction and surveillance

Each IBU is equipped with six small, fast and heavily armed boats, that are able to be deployed rapidly by air.

Inshore Boat Units are deployed on anti-terrorism and force protection duties in harbours and coastal waterways in the continental United States and at overseas locations such as Korea, the Gulf and the Horn of Africa region.

USS Makin Island

AMPHIBIOUS ASSAULT SHIPS (LHD/LHA)

WASP CLASS

Ship	Pennant Number	Comm Date	Builder
WASP	LHD 1	1989	Ingalls SB
ESSEX	LHD 2	1992	Ingalls SB
KEARSARGE	LHD 3	1993	Ingalls SB
BOXER	LHD 4	1995	Ingalls SB
BATAAN	LHD 5	1997	Ingalls SB
BONHOMME RICHARD	LHD 6	1998	Ingalls SB
IWO JIMA	LHD 7	2001	Ingalls SB
MAKIN ISLAND	LHD 8	2009	Ingalls SB

Machinery Two boilers; two geared steam turbines driving two shafts; 70,000shp **Displacement** 40,650 tons (LHD 1-4); 40,358 (LHD 5-7); 41,772 (LHD 8) **Dimensions**

257.3m x 32.3m x 8.1m **Speed** 22 knots **Armament** Two RAM launchers; two NATO Sea Sparrow launchers; three 20mm Phalanx CIWS mounts (two on LHD 5-7); four .50 cal. MG; four 25 mm Mk 38 MG (LHD 5-7 have three 25 mm Mk 38 MG) **Aircraft** 12 CH-46 Sea Knight helicopters; 4 CH-53E Sea Stallion helicopters; 6 AV-8B Harrier attack aircraft; 3 UH-1N Huey helicopters; 4 AH-1W Super Cobra helicopters **Complement** 1108 (+1894 Marines)

Notes

The largest of all amphibious warfare ships the LHD resembles a small aircraft carrier; capable of operating V/STOL aircraft, CV-22 Osprey tiltrotor and conventional helicopters. The ships also have a well deck in which three Landing Craft Air Cushion (LCAC) and other watercraft can be carried. These ships were the last major ships in the USN to be built with steam turbines. MAKIN ISLAND was completed with a gas turbine powerplant. They have extensive medical facilities comprising six fully equipped operating theatres and a 600 bed hospital.

The aircraft mix depends upon the ships mission, but it can include up to 42 CH-46 Sea Knight helicopters in the pure assault role or 20 AV-8B Harriers and 6 ASW helicopters in the Sea Control mission.

Traditionally USN amphibious ships deployed as part of an Amphibious Ready Group (ARG), which typically comprised an LHD or LHA, supported by LPDs and LSDs. The ARG would then come under the umbrella of a Carrier Battle Group. Under *Sea Power 21* deployment patterns changed and the Amphibious ships deployed as an Expeditionary Strike Group (ESG). This was still centred around the usual elements of an ARG, but now included their own escort and strike package comprising a guided missile cruiser armed with Tomahawk missiles, a guided missile destroyer, a frigate and a nuclear-powered submarine. There are indications, however, that the ESG may have given way once more to the ARG as recent deployments have dropped the ESG nomenclature in favour of ARG.

USS America

AMERICA CLASS

Ship	Pennant Number	Completion Date	Builder
AMERICA	LHA 6	*2013*	Ingalls SB

Machinery Two marine gas turbines, two shafts, 70,000 bhp, two 5,000 hp auxiliary propulsion motors. **Displacement** 44,971 long tons full load **Dimensions** 257.3m x 32.3m x 7.9m **Speed** 20+ knots **Armament** Two RAM launchers; two NATO Sea Sparrow launchers (with Evolved Sea Sparrow Missile (ESSM)); two 20mm Phalanx CIWS mounts; seven twin .50 cal. machine guns **Aircraft** F-35B Lightning (Joint Strike Fighter) STOVL aircraft; MV-22 Osprey VTOL tiltrotors; CH-53E Sea Stallion helicopters; UH-1Y Huey helicopters; AH-1Z Super Cobra helicopters; MH-60S Seahawk helicopters **Complement** 1,059 (Marine Detachment 1,687 plus 184 for surge operations).

Notes

Contracted for in 2007, LHA 6 will be an aviation-centric modified repeat of LHD 8 and is scheduled for delivery to the USN in 2013. Key differences between LHA 6 and the LHD class ships include an enlarged hangar deck, enhanced aviation maintenance facilities, increased aviation fuel capacity, additional aviation storerooms, removal of the well deck, and an electronically reconfigurable C4ISR suite. Long lead items for a second vessel were contracted for in 2010.

USS Nassau

TARAWA CLASS

Ship	Pennant Number	Completion Date	Builder
NASSAU	LHA 4	1978	Ingalls SB
PELELIU	LHA 5	1978	Ingalls SB

Machinery Two boilers; two geared steam turbines driving two shafts; 70,000shp
Displacement 39,400 tons **Dimensions** 249.9m x 31.8m x 7.9m **Speed** 24 knots
Armament Two RAM launchers; two Phalanx 20 mm CIWS mount; three .50 cal. MG;
four 25 mm Mk 38 MG **Aircraft** 2 CH-46 Sea Knight helicopters; 4 CH-53E Sea Stallion
helicopters; 6 AV-8B Harrier attack aircraft; 3 UH-1N Huey helicopters; 4 AH-1W Super
Cobra helicopters **Complement** 964 (Marine Detachment 1,900 plus).

Notes

These ships are to be replaced under the LHA(R) programme which is scheduled to
deliver the first ship in 2013. SAIPAN decommissioned in 2007 to be used for a series
of "experiments". TARAWA decommissioned in 2009 after which she was towed to
Hawaii where it is likely she will be sunk as a target. NASSAU was scheduled to decommission in 2011, but the USN is investigating a service life extension for the vessel. If not
economical the ship will be kept in a reserve status.

USS Mount Whitney

AMPHIBIOUS COMMAND SHIPS
BLUE RIDGE CLASS

Ship	Pennant Number	Completion Date	Builder
BLUE RIDGE	LCC 19	1970	Philadelphia Naval SY
MOUNT WHITNEY	LCC 20	1971	Newport News SB

Machinery Two boilers; one geared steam turbines driving one shaft; 22,000shp
Displacement 18,874 tons **Dimensions** 190m x 32m x 8.8m **Speed** 23 knots
Armament 2 x Phalanx CIWS **Complement** 842

Notes

As opposed to earlier Amphibious Command Ships which were conversions of earlier
vessels, these two ships were designed specifically for the role. Earlier amphibious
command ships lacked sufficient speed to keep up with a 20-knot amphibious force.
Both ships now serve as fleet flagships. BLUE RIDGE became the Seventh Fleet command ship in 1979, and MOUNT WHITNEY became the Second Fleet command ship
in 1981, and the Sixth Fleet command ship in February 2005. Although commanded by
a USN officer and having a USN mission crew, navigation, seamanship, engineering,
laundry and galley services are provided by Military Sealift Command civil service
mariners.

US NAVY/MCS2 JASON R. ZALASKY   **USS Mesa Verde**

AMPHIBIOUS TRANSPORT DOCK (LPD)

SAN ANTONIO CLASS

Ship	Pennant Number	Comm Date	Builder
SAN ANTONIO	LPD 17	2006	Northrop Grumman SS Avondale
NEW ORLEANS	LPD 18	2007	Northrop Grumman SS Avondale
MESA VERDE	LPD 19	2007	Northrop Grumman SS Pascagoula
GREEN BAY	LPD 20	2009	Northrop Grumman SS Avondale
NEW YORK	LPD 21	2009	Northrop Grumman SS Avondale
SAN DIEGO	LPD 22	2010	Northrop Grumman SS Pascagoula
ANCHORAGE	LPD 23	*2011*	Northrop Grumman SS Avondale
ARLINGTON	LPD 24	*2011*	Northrop Grumman SS Pascagoula
SOMERSET	LPD 25	*2011*	Northrop Grumman SS Avondale
JOHN P MURTHA	LPD 26	*Building*	Northrop Grumman SS Pascagoula

Machinery Four sequentially turbo-charged marine Colt-Pielstick diesels driving two shafts; 41,600shp **Displacement** 25,300 tonnes **Dimensions** 208.5m x 31.9m x 7m **Speed** 22+ knots **Armament** Two Bushmaster II 30 mm Close in Guns; two Rolling Airframe Missile launchers **Aircraft** Launch or land two CH53E Super Stallion helicopters or two MV-22 Osprey tilt-rotor aircraft or up to four CH-46 Sea Knight helicopters, AH-1 or UH-1 helicopters **Complement** 360 (Embarked landing force 720 - surge capacity to 800)

Notes

The 12-ship LPD 17 programme serves as the functional replacement for the Austin class LPD, Anchorage class LSD, Newport class LST and Charleston class LKA. The initial contract award to design and build the lead ship of the class was awarded to the Avondale-Bath Alliance in December 1996. A contract award protest was successfully resolved in April 1997. LPD 17 class workload was transferred from Bath Iron Works to Northrop Grumman Ship Systems (NGSS) in June 2002.

The ships have 25,000 square feet of space for vehicles (more than twice that of the Austin class), 34,000 cubic feet for cargo, accommodation for approximately 720 troops (800 surge), and a medical facility (24 beds and four operating rooms - two medical and two dental). The aft well deck can launch and recover traditional surface assault craft as well as two landing craft air cushion (LCAC) vehicles, capable of transporting cargo, personnel, Marine vehicles, and tanks, and the Marine Corps' new Expeditionary Fighting Vehicle (EFV). Aviation facilities include a hangar and flight deck (33 per cent larger than Austin class) in order to operate and maintain a variety of aircraft, including current and future rotary-wing aircraft. Other advanced features include the Advance Enclosed Mast/Sensor (AEM/S) for reduced signature/sensor maintenance, reduced-signature composite-material enclosed masts, other stealth enhancements, state-of-the-art C4ISR and self-defence systems, a Shipboard Wide-Area Network (SWAN) that will link shipboard systems and embarked Marine Corps units, and significant quality of life improvements for the ships company.

The programme has been plagued by reports of poor workmanship, late delivery and rising budgets. LPD 24 and LPD 25 are named ARLINGTON and SOMERSET respectively to honour the heroes and victims of the 11 September 2001 Pentagon attack and the flight downed in Pennsylvania. LPD 26 was named in April 2010 after the long serving Pennsylvania Democrat who chaired the House Appropriations Defence sub-committee.

On 20 October 2010 the US Navy awarded a $62 million cost plus fixed-fee advance procurement contract modification to Northrop Grumman Corporation that will provide long lead materials for LPD 27, the11th ship of the class.

USS Cleveland

AUSTIN CLASS

Ship	Pennant Number	Completion Date	Builder
CLEVELAND	LPD 7	1967	Ingalls SB
DUBUQUE	LPD 8	1967	Ingalls SB
DENVER	LPD 9	1968	Lockheed SB & Construction Co
PONCE	LPD 15	1971	Lockheed SB & Construction Co

Machinery Two boilers, two steam turbines driving two shafts; 24,000shp **Displacement** 17,272 tonnes **Dimensions** 171m x 25.2m x 7m **Speed** 21 knots **Armament** Two 25mm Mk 38 guns; two Phalanx CIWS; and eight .50-calibre MG **Aircraft** Up to six CH-46 Sea Knight helicopters **Complement** 420 (Marine Detachment 900)

Notes

The versatile Austin-class LPDs, a lengthened version of the earlier Raleigh class, provide substantial amphibious lift for USMC troops and their vehicles and cargo.

Additionally, they serve as the secondary aviation platform for Expeditionary Strike Groups, having a large flight deck capable of operating up to six CH-46 Sea Knight, or three CH-53 Sea Stallion helicopters. A small telescoping hangar, suitable only for a small utility helicopter, is fitted to all except AUSTIN. A well deck can accommodate one landing craft air cushion (LCAC), or one utility landing craft (LCU), or four mechanized landing craft (LCU). Ships can accommodate up to 900 troops and carry 2,000 tons of supplies and equipment. LPD-7 to LPD-13 have an extra superstructure level enabling them to operate as flagships. All are to be replaced by the San Antonio class LPD.

DUBUQUE and CLEVELAND are to decommission in 2011 and to be kept in a reserve status.

USS Ashland

WHIDBEY ISLAND CLASS

Ship	Pennant Number	Completion Date	Builder
WHIDBEY ISLAND	LSD 41	1985	Lockheed SB & Construction Co
GERMANTOWN	LSD 42	1986	Lockheed SB & Construction Co
FORT McHENRY	LSD 43	1987	Lockheed SB & Construction Co
GUNSTON HALL	LSD 44	1989	Avondale Industries
COMSTOCK	LSD 45	1990	Avondale Industries
TORTUGA	LSD 46	1990	Avondale Industries
RUSHMORE	LSD 47	1991	Avondale Industries
ASHLAND	LSD 48	1992	Avondale Industries

Machinery Four Colt Industries, 16 Cylinder diesels driving two shafts; 33,000shp
Displacement 15, 726 tonnes **Dimensions** 185.6m x 25.6m x 6.3m **Speed** 20+ knots

Armament Two 25mm Mk 38 MG; Two 20mm Phalanx CIWS mounts and Six .50 cal. MG **Landing Craft** Four Landing Craft Air Cushion (LCAC) **Complement** 413 (Marine Detachment 402 plus 102 surge)

Notes

The LSD 41 class was designed specifically to operate Landing Craft Air Cushion (LCAC) vessels - basically gas turbine powered cargo-carrying hovercraft - and it has the largest capacity for these landing craft (four) of any USN amphibious ship. The ships can ballast down in 15 minutes and deballast in 30, providing a depth of water of 6ft forward and 10 foot aft for operating landing craft. The flight deck is raised above the 440 ft long docking well in order to provide all-around ventilation for the gas turbine-engined LCACs. There are two landing spots on the flight deck for up to CH-53-sized helicopters but no hangar facilities. The ships carry 90 tons JP-5 fuel for helicopters. Medical facilities include an operating room and 8 beds. In an effort to enhance the ship's ability to counter the cruise missile threat Phalanx CIWS and RAM missile systems are being progressively fitted throughout the class.

USS Pearl Harbor

DOCK LANDING SHIP (LSD)
HARPERS FERRY CLASS

Ship	Pennant Number	Commission Date	Builder
HARPERS FERRY	LSD 49	1995	Avondale Industries
CARTER HALL	LSD 50	1995	Avondale Industries
OAK HILL	LSD 51	1996	Avondale Industries
PEARL HARBOR	LSD 52	1998	Avondale Industries

Machinery Four Colt Industries, 16 Cylinder diesels driving two shafts; 33,000shp **Displacement** 16,976 tonnes **Dimensions** 185.6m x 25.6m x 6.3m **Speed** 20+ knots **Armament** Two 25mm Mk 38 MF, Two 20mm Phalanx CIWS mounts and Six .50 cal. MG **Landing Craft** Two Landing Craft Air Cushion (LCAC) **Complement** 419 (Marine Detachment 402 plus 102 surge)

Notes
Similar in all respects to the Whidbey Island class, these four vessels were optimised for the cargo carrying role. The ships differ from the original LSD 41 by reducing the number of LCACs to two in favour of additional cargo capacity. The well deck has been shortened and the portside crane removed.

LCAC-67

LANDING CRAFT AIR CUSHION (LCAC)

Machinery 4x Allied-Signal TF-40B gas turbines (2 for propulsion/2 for lift); 16,000 hp sustained; 2 x shrouded reversible pitch airscrews; 4 x double-entry fans, centrifugal or mixed flow (lift); 4 x Vericor Power Systems ETF-40B gas turbines with Full Authority Digital Engine Control (FADEC) **Displacement** 185 tonnes **Dimensions** 26.4m x 14.3m **Speed** 40+ knots **Armament**   12.7mm MGs. Gun mounts will support: M2HB .50 cal machine gun; Mk 19 Mod3 40mm grenade launcher; M60 MG **Range** 200 miles at 40 kts with payload / 300 miles at 35 kts with payload **Load** 60 tons / 75 ton overload **Military Lift** 24 troops or 1 Main Battle Tank **Complement** 5

Notes

91 LCACs were built between 1984 and 2001, production being split between Textron Marine and Land Systems and Avondale Gulfport Marine. The LCAC is a high-speed, over-the-beach fully amphibious landing craft, capable of carrying a 60-75 ton payload. It is used to transport the weapons systems, equipment, cargo and personnel of the assault elements of the Marine Air-Ground Task Force from ship to shore and across the beach. Its air cushion design allows it to access more than 70% of the world's coastline. LCACs are transported in, and can be deployed from, any USN amphibious ship equipped with a well deck. In recent years these craft have proven themselves invaluable in providing humanitarian relief to areas devastated by tsunami and hurricane, being able to access remote areas. A Service Life Extension Programme (SLEP) to extend hull life from 20 to 30 years for 73 of the 82 active LCACs will be accomplished through 2017. Nine craft that were in reduced operating status were deleted in 2006. A replacement programme, imaginatively titled the Seabase to Shore Connector (SSC), is expected to deliver a vessel capable of lifting 73 tons by 2015.

LCU-1655

LANDING CRAFT
UTILITY (LCU) 1600 CLASS

Machinery 2 x Detroit 12V-71 Diesel engines, twin shaft, 680 hp sustained, Kort nozzles **Displacement** 381 tonnes **Dimensions** 41.1m x 8.8m x 2m **Speed** 12 knots **Armament** 12.7mm MGs **Range** 190 miles at 9 kts with full load **Load** 180 tons **Military Lift** 125 tons of cargo **Complement** 14

Notes

Powered by two diesel engines driving twin shafts, LCUs are able to transport tracked or wheeled vehicles and troops from amphibious assault ships to beachheads or piers and have both bow and stern ramps for onload/offload at either end. The LCU 1600 class were built from the 1960's through to the 1980's and are still used to transport those loads too heavy for the LCACs, being able to transport up to three M-60 tanks or 400 troops. LCUs are also able to operate independently of their mother ships and are equipped with accommodation spaces for the crew. Similar craft are operated by the US Army.

JOINT HIGH SPEED VESSEL

Ship	Pennant Number	Commission Date	Builder
SPEARHEAD	JHSV 1	*2011*	Bollinger/IncatUSA
VIGILANT	JHSV 2	*2012*	Bollinger/IncatUSA
FORTITUDE	JHSV 3	*2012*	Bollinger/IncatUSA
FALL RIVER	JHSV 4	*Buiding*	Bollinger/IncatUSA

Machinery 4 x MTU 20V8000 M71L Diesels; 4 x Wartsila WLD 1400 SR Waterjets
Displacement Dwt **Dimensions** 103m x 28.5m x 3.83m **Speed** Average 35 knots (43 knots without payload) **Range** 1200 miles (max transit); 5600 miles (self-deployment) **Load** 635 MT **Aircraft** CH-53E capable flight deck **Complement** 41

Notes

The JHSV programme is a joint effort between the Army and the Navy to acquire ten high-speed vessels for the two branches of the US military. JHSV will be used for fast intra-theatre transportation of troops, military vehicles and equipment. They will be capable of transporting 700 short tons 1,200 nautical miles at an average speed of 35 knots, and can operate in shallow-draft ports and waterways, interfacing with roll-on/roll-off discharge facilities, and on/off-loading a combat-loaded Abrams Main Battle Tank (M1A2). Other joint requirements include an aviation flight deck to support day and night air vehicle launch and recovery operations. Also, JHSV will have airline style seating for 312 embarked troops and fixed berthing for 104 more. Original announcements indicated that JHSV-1 would be FORTITUDE, but at the keel-laying she was named SPEARHEAD.

HSV Swift

HIGH SPEED VESSEL

Ship	Pennant Number	Commission Date	Builder
SWIFT	HSV 2	2003	Bollinger/IncatUSA

Machinery Caterpillar 3618 marine Diesel engines **Displacement** 700 Dwt **Dimensions** 98m x 27m x 3.4m **Speed** 45+ knots **Armament** 25mm Mk 96 gun **Range** 4000+ miles **Load** 605 tons **Complement** 42

Notes

A high-speed catamaran, SWIFT has been chartered by Military Sealift Command. Drawing on experience gained from JOINT VENTURE (HSV-X1) and the Army's high-speed theatre support vessel SPEARHEAD (TSV-1X), SWIFT will be used to develop concepts in support of the Littoral Combat Ship (LCS) programme. SWIFT has recently deployed to the Mediterranean, Africa and Far East on both humanitarian and operational operations.

EXPERIMENTAL CRAFT
SEA FIGHTER

Ship	Pennant Number	Completion Date	Builder
SEA FIGHTER	FSF-1	2005	Nichols Brothers Boat Builders

Machinery Two GE LM2500 Gas Turbines; two MTU diesels driving four Rolls-Royce waterjets **Displacement** 950 tons **Dimensions** 79.9m x 22m x 3.5m **Speed** 50+ knots **Complement** 26

Notes

The Littoral Surface Craft-Experimental LSC(X) was developed by the Office of Naval Research and christened SEA FIGHTER (FSF-1) on 5 February 2005. This high speed aluminum catamaran will test a variety of technologies that will allow the USN to operate in littoral waters. Following approximately two months of trials, SEA FIGHTER was delivered at the end of April 2005. Operational control rests with the USN's Third Fleet with the ship operating out of San Diego, CA. SEA FIGHTER is used to evaluate the hydrodynamic performance, structural behaviour, mission flexibility, and propulsion system efficiency of high speed vessels.

USS Emory S. Land

SUBMARINE TENDERS
L.Y. SPEAR CLASS

Ship	Pennant Number	Completion Date	Builder
EMORY S. LAND	AS 39	1979	Lockheed SB & Construction Co
FRANK CABLE	AS 40	1980	Lockheed SB & Construction Co

Machinery Two boilers; two geared steam turbines driving one shaft; 20,000shp
Displacement 23,493 tonnes **Dimensions** 196.2m x 25.9m x 8.7m **Speed** 20 knots
Armament Four 20mm Mk 67 Oerlikon **Complement** 587 (plus 94 Flag Staff)

Notes

The L.Y. Spear class is designed and equipped to support nuclear-powered attack submarines and can service up to four submarines berthed alongside simultaneously. The
ship's capabilities include: nuclear system repair and testing, electrical and electronic
repair, hull repair, sheet metal and steel work, pipe fabrication, foundry, woodworking,
underwater diving and rescue, and hazardous material management. Various services
are available to all submarines alongside including steam, diesel fuel, water, and elec-
tricity. The ships are capable of handling and storing submarine launched weapons. In
addition they provide living quarters for more than 1500 people and are equipped with
full medical and dental facilities, laundry and dry cleaning plants, data processing equipment and large storage areas for refrigerated and dry cargo food. They have one 30 ton
crane and two mobile cranes. AS 40 is forward deployed at Guam. With the closure of
the base at La Maddalena, Italy, AS 39 returned to Bremerton for overhaul in 2007. She
was transferred to the Military Sealift Command in 2010, though still under the command
of a USN Commanding Officer, and forward deployed to Diego Garcia.

YP 684

YARD PATROL CRAFT

Machinery Two Detroit 12V-71 diesels driving two shafts; 680shp **Displacement** 167 tons FL **Dimensions** 32.9m x 7.3m x 2.4m **Speed** 13 knots **Complement** 6 (plus 24 Trainees/Midshipmen)

Notes

Used for training and research purposes, twenty three of these small vessels were built from the 1980s (21 are operated by the Naval Academy and two by the Office of Naval Research). The YPs are used to teach familiarisation with water craft, Basic Damage Control and at-sea instruction of Basic to Advanced Seamanship and Navigation. Training is also undertaken in navigation and seamanship for midshipmen at the US Naval Academy in Annapolis, Maryland, and candidates at Officer Candidate School, Pensacola, Florida.

A new class of YPC is under construction (YP 703-709) designed to emphasise habit-ability, training areas, hull structure, integrated bridge, maneuverability, propulsion plant configuration, and, for training purposes only, simulated Underway Replenishment.

USS Constitution

HISTORIC FLAGSHIP

Ship	Completion Date	Builder
CONSTITUTION	1797	Edmond Hartt's Shipyard, Boston

Propulsion 42,710 sq. ft of sail on three masts **Displacement** 2,200 tonnes **Dimensions** 62m (53m at waterline) x 13.3m x 4.4m **Speed** 13+ knots **Complement** 450 including 55 Marines and 30 boys (1797)

Notes

USS CONSTITUTION is a fully-commissioned US Naval vessel, and is the oldest commissioned warship afloat in the world. Although she is duly recognised and honoured, she holds no official 'flagship' status, though the term is frequently used honourarily. Today she acts in the capacity of the USN's ambassador to the public. Based at Boston, the ship has about 55 active-duty USN crewmembers. About 25 Navy-employed civilians (the Naval Historical Centre, Detachment Boston) perform the in-depth and ongoing maintenance of the ship. Her last major restoration period was in the early 1990's in preparation for the '97 Sail,' the first time she sailed under her own sail power in 116 years. Each year she is taken out into the bay and turned to prevent her masts warping in the prevailing weather.

MILITARY SEALIFT COMMAND

During World War II, four separate government agencies controlled sea transportation. In 1949, the Military Sea Transportation Service, renamed Military Sealift Command (MSC) in 1970, became the single managing agency for the Department of Defence's ocean transportation needs.

From that day on MSC has provided ocean transportation of equipment, fuel, supplies and ammunition to sustain US forces worldwide during peacetime and in war. During a war, more than 95 percent of all equipment and supplies needed by US military forces overseas would be carried by sea.

MSC operates more than 120 ships worldwide on a day-to-day basis and, if needed, has access to more than 100 ships usually kept in a reduced operating status in US ports.

Today, MSC has more than 10,800 employees worldwide, approximately 80 percent of which serve at sea. MSC is the largest employer of merchant mariners in the United States. Approximately 5,100 employees are federal civil service, 660 are military personnel; and another 4,600 are employed by MSC contractors. All MSC ships, unlike other US Navy ships, are crewed by civilians. Some ships have small military departments assigned to carry out communication, supply and aviation functions.

The MSC is organised around four core programmes.

NAVAL FLEET AUXILIARY FORCE PROGRAMME

The Naval Fleet Auxiliary Force provides the bulk of the USN's combat logistics services, the equivalent to the British Royal Fleet Auxiliary. MSC has 42 NFAF ships, that are government-owned vessels, but crewed by civil service mariners - many of the ships were previously USN manned and operated, but have been transferred to MSC operation with considerable operational cost savings. Small Navy departments that previously handled communications and signaling have been replaced by civilian mariners. A similar programme will replace some Navy supply personnel with civilians aboard MSC's five combat stores ships. The NFAF comprises Combat Support ships, Fleet Replenishment oilers and Dry Cargo/Ammunition ships. Providing fuel, food, ammunition, spare parts and other supplies, NFAF ships enable the USN fleet to remain at sea, on station and combat ready. In addition to delivering supplies at sea, NFAF also operate salvage ships and Fleet tugs for towing and salvage operations. The two Hospital Ships, MERCY and COMFORT are also operated under the NFAF programme.

SPECIAL MISSION PROGRAMME

The Special Mission Programme provides unique vessels and services for a variety of US military and federal government missions. Specialized services include oceanographic and hydrographic surveys, underwater surveillance, missile tracking, acoustic surveys and submarine support.

MSC's Special Mission Programme controls 25 ships supporting several different USN customers, including the Naval Sea Systems Command and the Oceanographer of the Navy. Both civil service and contractor-employed mariners operate these vessels. Technical work, survey operations and communications are conducted by embarked military personnel, civilian scientists and related technicians. Special mission ships average 25 days at sea and five days in port each month.

Oceanographic survey ships study the world's oceans using multi-beam, wide-angle, precision hydrographic sonar systems to collect bathymetric data. Four of the five ocean surveillance ships work directly with the Navy's fleets, listening for undersea threats.

MSC operates one cable-laying ship which transports, deploys, retrieves and repairs submarine cables. ZEUS was built specifically for the Navy; the ship can lay up to 1,000 miles of cable in depths of 9,000 feet during a single deployment before having to restock its cable supply.

Missile range instrumentation ships provide platforms for monitoring missile launches and collecting data which can be used to improve missile efficiency and accuracy. OBSERVATION ISLAND monitors compliance with strategic arms treaties and supports US military weapons test programmes.She will soon be replaced by HOWARD O. LORENZEN, currently under construction and due to enter service in 2011. Other ships provide communication, flight safety, photographic coverage and missile tracking capabilities in support of fleet ballistic missile flight tests.

In addition to its government-owned ships, the Special Mission Programme is responsible for seven chartered vessels. Two ships provide deep submergence/salvage support and submarine/escort rescue assistance for the Navy's submarine forces. One ship supports the Naval Special Warfare Command. Four other ships were chartered in 2007 to support the Navy's submarine escort requirements while entering and leaving ports.

PREPOSITIONING PROGRAMME

The Prepositioning Programme strategically places military equipment and supplies aboard ships in key ocean areas for the US Army, Marine Corps, Air Force, Defence Logistics Agency and Navy. Prepositioning ships remain at sea, ready on short notice to deliver vital equipment, fuel and supplies to support US military forces in the event of a major theatre war, humanitarian operation or other contingency. MSC prepositioning ships are located in three strategic areas: the Mediterranean and eastern Atlantic Ocean, the Indian Ocean and the western Pacific Ocean. The Prepositioning Programme consists of 32 at-sea ships plus 2 aviation support ships kept in reduced operating status. They include long-term chartered commercial vessels, activated Ready Reserve Force ships, and US government-owned ships. All are crewed by mariners provided by companies under contract to MSC.

While most active ships in MSC's Prepositioning Programme strategically place combat gear at sea, there are other ships, including: Two high-speed vessels that transport Marines, their combat vehicles and their associated gear in and around the Far East; A chartered offshore petroleum distribution system ship that can deliver fuel from up to eight miles offshore; and Two aviation logistics support ships that are activated as needed from reduced operating status to provide at-sea maintenance for Marine Corps fixed- and rotary-wing aircraft.

The ships are organised into three squadrons: MPS Squadron One, usually located in the Mediterranean and eastern Atlantic; MPS Squadron Two, usually located at Diego Garcia in the Indian Ocean; and MPS Squadron Three, normally in the Guam/Saipan area.

Each squadron carries sufficient equipment and supplies to sustain about 15,000 Marine Corps Air Ground Task Force personnel for up to 30 days. Each ship can discharge cargo either alongside or while anchored offshore using barges carried aboard. Beginning in 2000, three Maritime Prepositioning Force (Enhanced) ships were added into the existing MPS squadrons, one ship per squadron, to provide critical new capabilities for the Marine Corps. Each MPF(E) ship carries a Navy fleet hospital, an expeditionary airfield and engineering equipment.

The Logistics Prepositioning Force operates ten vessels for the USN, the Defence Logistics Agency and the US Air Force.

The Air Force prepositioned fleet consists of munitions carriers such as MV CAPT STEVEN L. BENNETT, MV TSGT JOHN A. CHAPMAN, MV MAJ BERNARD F FISHER and MV A1C WILLIAM H PITSENBARGER.

For Navy prepositioning, MSC operates modular cargo delivery system (MCDS) vessels like SS CAPE JACOB. The vessels carry naval ordnance and also have the capability to operate as shuttle replenishment ships for naval battle groups.

SEALIFT PROGRAMME

The Sealift Programme provides ocean transportation for the Department of Defence and other government agencies using commercially chartered and government-owned dry cargo ships and tankers. Sealift ships carry DoD cargo to ports not served by regularly scheduled US commercial ocean going vessels. MSC also has access to the US Maritime Administration's Ready Reserve Force.

The Sealift Programme comprises, Tanker, Dry Cargo and Surge Project Offices each ensuring availabilty of suitable shipping.

The heart of the MSC tanker fleet are three Champion-class, double-hulled, ice-strengthened tankers built in 1985. These tankers are government owned and contract operated.

The Dry Cargo Project Office handles all Department of Defence cargo requirements that cannot be accommodated by regularly scheduled ocean liner service. Nearly all peacetime DoD cargo is shipped via US flagged contracted or government-owned ships. During a military contingency, additional vessels may be chartered to expand sealift capabilities to meet additional demand.

The Surge Project Office manages strategic sealift ships that can be activated from reduced operating status to support the US military in exercises, contingencies and war.

MSC's large, medium-speed, roll-on/roll-off ships, or LMSRs, are among the largest cargo ships in the world and can carry up to 380,000 square feet of combat cargo - the equivalent of more than six football fields of wheeled and tracked vehicles - at speeds up to 24 knots. LMSRs are equipped with on board ramps and cranes to assist in loading oversize cargo including helicopters, M1A1 tanks and Bradley armoured personnel carriers. MSC operates eleven surge LMSRs using commercial operating companies to crew and maintain the ships as necessary in order to be ready to sail within 96 hours of notification.

Ready Reserve Force ships are owned and maintained by the US Department of Transportation's Maritime Administration (MARAD) at strategic locations around the US coasts near Army loading ports. Normally kept in four-, five-, 10- or 20-day reduced operating status, the 59 militarily useful ships come under MSC control when activated. Ships may be activated for humanitarian operations, military exercises and contingencies and for war. The RRF includes tankers, crane ships, roll-on/roll-off ships, heavy lift ships, lighter-aboard-ship vessels and modular cargo delivery system ships. During Operation Iraqi Freedom thirty-three RRF ships were directly involved, delivering more than nine million square feet of combat cargo for US forces in Iraq. RRF ships can be recognised by red, white and blue stripes around their funnel.

SHIPS OF THE MILITARY SEALIFT COMMAND
Pennant Numbers

Ship	Pennant Number	Ship	Pennant Number
NAVAL FLEET AUXILIARY FORCE		RICHARD E. BYRD	T-AKE 4
		ROBERT E. PEARY	T-AKE 5
Ammunition Ship		AMELIA EARHART	T-AKE 6
		CARL BRASHEAR	T-AKE 7
SHASTA	T-AE 33	WALLY SCHIRRA	T-AKE 8
KISKA	T-AE 35	MATTHEW PERRY	T-AKE 9
		CHARLES DREW	T-AKE 10
Fast Combat Support Ship		WASHINGTON CHAMBERS	T-AKE 11
		WILLIAM McLEAN	T-AKE 12
SUPPLY	T-AOE 6	MEDGAR EVERS	T-AKE 13
RAINIER	T-AOE 7	*NOT YET NAMED*	T-AKE 14
ARCTIC	T-AOE 8		
BRIDGE	T-AOE 10	**Hospital Ship**	
		MERCY	T-AH 19
Fleet Replenishment Oiler		COMFORT	T-AH 20
HENRY J. KAISER	T-AO 187		
JOSHUA HUMPHREYS	T-AO 188	**Rescue-Salvage Ship**	
JOHN LENTHALL	T-AO 189		
WALTER S. DIEHL	T-AO 193	SAFEGUARD	T-ARS 50
JOHN ERICSSON	T-AO 194	GRASP	T-ARS 51
LEROY GRUMMAN	T-AO 195	SALVOR	T-ARS 52
KANAWHA	T-AO 196	GRAPPLE	T-ARS 53
PECOS	T-AO 197		
BIG HORN	T-AO 198	**Fleet Ocean Tug**	
TIPPECANOE	T-AO 199		
GUADALUPE	T-AO 200	CATAWBA	T-ATF 168
PATUXENT	T-AO 201	NAVAJO	T-ATF 169
YUKON	T-AO 202	SIOUX	T-ATF 171
LARAMIE	T-AO 203	APACHE	T-ATF 172
RAPPAHANNOCK	T-AO 204		
		SPECIAL MISSION SHIPS	
Dry Cargo/Ammunition Ship			
		Missile Range Instrumentation Ship	
LEWIS AND CLARK	T-AKE 1		
SACAGAWEA	T-AKE 2	OBSERVATION ISLAND	T-AGM 23
ALAN SHEPARD	T-AKE 3		

Ship	Pennant Number	Ship	Pennant Number
INVINCIBLE	T-AGM 24	**SEALIFT SHIPS**	
HOWARD O LORENZEN	T-AGM 25		
		LMSR	
Ocean Surveillance Ship			
		SHUGHART	T-AKR 295
VICTORIOUS	T-AGOS 19	GORDON	T-AKR 296
ABLE	T-AGOS 20	YANO	T-AKR 297
EFFECTIVE	T-AGOS 21	GILLILAND	T-AKR 298
LOYAL	T-AGOS 22	BOB HOPE	T-AKR 300
IMPECCABLE	T-AGOS 23	FISHER	T-AKR 301
		SEAY	T-AKR 302
Oceanographic Survey Ship		MENDONCA	T-AKR 303
		PILILAAU	T-AKR 304
PATHFINDER	T-AGS 60	BRITTIN	T-AKR 305
SUMNER	T-AGS 61	BENAVIDEZ	T-AKR 306
BOWDITCH	T-AGS 62		
HENSON	T-AGS 63	**Government-owned Tanker**	
BRUCE C. HEEZEN	T-AGS 64		
MARY SEARS	T-AGS 65	PAUL BUCK	T-AOT 1122
NOT YET NAMED	T-AGS 66	RICHARD G. MATTHIESEN	
			T-AOT 1124
Navigation Test Support Ship		LAWRENCE H. GIANELLA	
			T-AOT 1125
WATERS	T-AGS 45		
		Long Term Government Charter	
Cable Repair Ship			
		MV AMERICAN TERN	T-AK 4729
ZEUS	T-ARC 7	MV MOHEGAN	T-AK 5158
		MV TRANSPACIFIC	T-1 TANKER
Submarine & Special Warfare Support Vessel		MV VIRGINIAN	T-AK 9205
		PREPOSITIONING SHIPS	
SSV C-CHAMPION			
SSV C-COMMANDO		**LMSRs**	
MV DOLORES CHOUEST			
MV HOS BLUEWATER		WATSON	T-AKR 310
MV HOS GEMSTONE		SISLER	T-AKR 311
MV HOS GREYSTONE		DAHL	T-AKR 312
MV HOS SILVERSTAR		RED CLOUD	T-AKR 313

Ship	Pennant Number	Ship	Pennant Number
CHARLTON	T-AKR 314	**Offshore Petroleum Delivery Ship**	
WATKINS	T-AKR 315		
POMEROY	T-AKR 316	VADM K R WHEELER	T-AG 5001
SODERMAN	T-AKR 317		
		Aviation Maintenance Logistics Ships	
Container Ships			
CAPT STEVEN L. BENNETT		WRIGHT	T-AVB 3
	T-AK 4296	CURTISS	T-AVB 4
MAJ BERNARD F FISHER			
	T-AK 4396	**High-Speed Vessel**	
LTC JOHN U. D. PAGE	T-AK 4543		
		WESTPAC EXPRESS	HSV-4676
SSG EDWARD A. CARTER			
	T-AK 4544	**READY RESERVE FORCE SHIPS**	
Container & Roll-on/Roll-off Ships		**Fast Sealift Ship**	
TSGT JOHN A. CHAPMAN		ALGOL	T-AKR 287
	T-AK 323	BELLATRIX	T-AKR 288
SGT MATEJ KOCAK	T-AK 3005	DENEBOLA	T-AKR 289
PFC EUGENE A. O'BREGON		POLLUX	T-AKR 290
	T-AK 3006	ALTAIR	T-AKR 291
MAJ STEPHEN W. PLESS		REGULUS	T-AKR 292
	T-AK 3007	CAPELLA	T-AKR 293
2ND LT JOHN P. BOBO		ANTARES	T-AKR 294
	T-AK 3008		
PFC DEWAYNE T. WILLIAMS		**Modular Cargo Delivery System**	
	T-AK 3009		
1ST LT BALDOMERO LOPEZ		CAPE JACOB	T-AK 5029
	T-AK 3010		
1ST LT JACK LUMMUS		**Lighter Aboard Ships**	
	T-AK 3011		
SGT WILLIAM R. BUTTON		CAPE FLATTERY	T-AK 5070
	T-AK 3012	CAPE FAREWELL	T-AK 5073
1ST LT HARRY L. MARTIN			
	T-AK 3015	**Roll-on/Roll-off Ships**	
LCPL ROY M. WHEAT			
	T-AK 3016	CAPE ISLAND	T-AKR 10
GYSGT FRED W. STOCKHAM		CAPE INTREPID	T-AKR 11
	T-AK 3017	CAPE TEXAS	T-AKR 112

Ship	Pennant Number	Ship	Pennant Number
CAPE TAYLOR	T-AKR 113	CAPE RACE	T-AKR 9960
ADM WM. M. CALLAGHAN		CAPE WASHINGTON	T-AKR 9961
	T-AKR 1001	CAPE WRATH	T-AKR 9962
CAPE ORLANDO	T-AKR 2044		
CAPE DUCATO	T-AKR 5051	**Heavy Lift Ships**	
CAPE DOUGLAS	T-AKR 5052		
CAPE DOMINGO	T-AKR 5053	CAPE MAY	T-AKR 5063
CAPE DECISION	T-AKR 5054	CAPE MOHICAN	T-AKR 5065
CAPE DIAMOND	T-AKR 5055		
CAPE ISABEL	T-AKR 5062	**Government-owned Tankers**	
CAPE HUDSON	T-AKR 5066		
CAPE HENRY	T-AKR 5067	PETERSBURG	T-AOT 9101
CAPE HORN	T-AKR 5068		
CAPE EDMONT	T-AKR 5069	**Crane Ships**	
CAPE INSCRIPTION	T-AKR 5076		
CAPE KNOX	T-AKR 5082	KEYSTONE STATE	T-ACS 1
CAPE KENNEDY	T-AKR 5083	GEM STATE	T-ACS 2
CAPE VINCENT	T-AKR 9666	GRAND CANYON STATE	
CAPE RISE	T-AKR 9678		T-ACS 3
CAPE RAY	T-AKR 9679	GOPHER STATE	T-ACS 4
CAPE VICTORY	T-AKR 9701	FLICKERTAIL STATE	T-ACS 5
CAPE TRINITY	T-AKR 9711	CORNHUSKER STATE	T-ACS 6

USNS Shasta

AMMUNITION SHIPS
KILAUEA CLASS

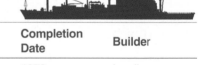

Ship	Pennant Number	Completion Date	Builder
SHASTA	T-AE 33	1972	Ingalls
KISKA	T-AE 35	1972	Ingalls

Machinery 3 Foster-Wheeler boilers; 1 GE turbine driving 1 shaft **Displacement** 19,940 tonnes (Full Load) **Dimensions** 171.9 x 24.7 x 8.5m **Speed** 20 knots **Armament** None **Aircraft** 2 x CH-46E Sea Knight or CH-60 Seahawks **Complement** 125-133 civilian (plus 7-24 military)

Notes

Former USN ships transferred to the MSC (KISKA 1996 and SHASTA 1997). They provide underway replenishment of all types of ammunition via heavy jackstay and vertical replenishment. Both will decommission in 2011.

USNS Rainier

FAST COMBAT SUPPORT SHIPS

SUPPLY CLASS

Ship	Pennant Number	Completion Date	Builder
SUPPLY	T-AOE 6	1994	NASSCo SD
RAINIER	T-AOE 7	1995	NASSCo SD
ARCTIC	T-AOE 8	1995	NASSCo SD
BRIDGE	T-AOE 10	1997	NASSCo SD

Machinery Four GE LM2500 gas-turbines driving two shafts; 105,000shp **Displacement** 49,583 tonnes **Dimensions** 229.9m x 32m x 11.6m **Speed** 25 knots **Aircraft** 3 x CH-46E Sea Knight helicopters **Complement** 160 civilians (59 military)

Notes

Transferred from the USN between 2001-04, these high speed vessels are the largest combat logistics ships in the MSC. These ships have the speed to keep up with the carrier groups and are able to resupply fuel, lubricants, dry stores and ammunition.

USNS Yukon

FLEET REPLENISHMENT OILER

HENRY J. KAISER CLASS

Ship	Pennant Number	Completion Date	Builder
HENRY J. KAISER	T-AO 187	1986	Avondale
JOSHUA HUMPHREYS	T-AO 188	1987	Avondale
JOHN LENTHALL	T-AO 189	1987	Avondale
WALTER S DIEHL	T-AO 193	1988	Avondale
JOHN ERICSSON	T-AO 194	1991	Avondale
LEROY GRUMMAN	T-AO 195	1989	Avondale
KANAWHA	T-AO 196	1991	Avondale
PECOS	T-AO 197	1990	Avondale
BIG HORN	T-AO 198	1992	Avondale
TIPPECANOE	T-AO 199	1993	Avondale

Ship	Pennant Number	Completion Date	Builder
GUADALUPE	T-AO 200	1992	Avondale
PATUXENT	T-AO 201	1995	Avondale
YUKON	T-AO 202	1993	Avondale
LARAMIE	T-AO 203	1996	Avondale
RAPPAHANNOCK	T-AO 204	1995	Avondale

Machinery 2 Colt-Pielstick 10 PC4.2 V 570 diesels driving 2 shafts; Controllable Pitch propellors **Displacement** 42,674 tonnes **Dimensions** 206.5m x 29.7m x 4m **Speed** 20 knots **Complement** 66-89 civilian (7-24 military)

Notes

Fitted with medium-speed diesel propulsion, the delivery of PATUXENT, RAPPAHANNOCK and LARAMIE were delayed by the decision to fit double hulls to meet the requirements of the Oil Pollution Act of 1990. This modification increased construction time from 32 to 42 months and reduced cargo capacity by 17 percent, although this can be restored in an emergency. Hull separation is 1.83 m at the sides and 1.98 m on the bottom.

Both HENRY J. KAISER and JOSHUA HUMPHREYS had been in long term lay up, the former at Diego Garcia since 2003 at reduced operational status. JOSHUA HUMPHREYS was placed in reserve in 1996 and briefly reactivated from February 2005 to October 2006. In March 2010 Atlantic Marine in Philadelphia was awarded a contract for the reactivation of the ship. In May 2010 the ship joined the US Fifth Fleet in support of counter-piracy and counter-terrorism operations in the Indian Ocean and Gulf area.

ANDREW J. HIGGINS (T-AO 190) was transferred to Chile in 2009 and commissioned as ALMIRANTE MONTT in 2010.

USNS Robert E Peary

AUXILIARY DRY CARGO SHIPS
LEWIS AND CLARK CLASS

Ship	Pennant Number	Completion Date	Builder
LEWIS AND CLARK	T-AKE 1	2006	GD NASSCo
SACAGAWEA	T-AKE 2	2007	GD NASSCo
ALAN SHEPARD	T-AKE 3	2007	GD NASSCo
RICHARD E. BYRD	T-AKE 4	2007	GD NASSCo
ROBERT E. PEARY	T-AKE 5	2008	GD NASSCo
AMELIA EARHART	T-AKE 6	2008	GD NASSCo
CARL BRASHEAR	T-AKE 7	2009	GD NASSCo
WALLY SCHIRRA	T-AKE 8	2009	GD NASSCo
MATTHEW PERRY	T-AKE 9	2010	GD NASSCo
CHARLES DREW	T-AKE 10	2010	GD NASSCo
WASHINGTON CHAMBERS	T-AKE 11	2010	GD NASSCo
WILLIAM McLEAN	T-AKE 12	2011	GD NASSCo
MEDGAR EVERS	T-AKE 13	2012	GD NASSCo
UN-NAMED	T-AKE 14	2012	GD NASSCo

Machinery Integrated propulsion and ship service electrical distribution system; Four FM/MAN diesel generators with total installed power of 35.7 MW. Twin synchronous, variable speed, reversible, double-wound, Alstom propulsion motors mounted in tandem,

Single fixed-pitch propeller **Displacement** 40,945 tons **Dimensions** 210m x 32.31m x 9m **Speed** 20 knots **Complement** 123 civilian (plus 49 military)

Notes

This class are replacing the remaining Kilauea-class ammunition ships, and the decommissoned Mars and Sirius-class combat stores ships, and when operating in concert with a Henry J. Kaiser-class (T-AO 187) oiler, they are replacements for the Sacramento-class (AOE) fast combat support ship. The T-AKE Programme consists of 14 ships and is scheduled to complete in 2012.

T-AKEs 12, 13 and 14 will each be assigned to one of the three active Maritime Prepositioning Ship squadrons, which are permanently forward deployed to the Eastern Atlantic Ocean/Mediterranean Sea, Western Pacific Ocean and Indian Ocean. While identical in configuration to T-AKEs 1-11, the mission of the last three ships in the class will be to provide selective offload of cargo for resupply and sustainment of US Marine Corps forces ashore.

USNS Mercy

HOSPITAL SHIPS
MERCY CLASS

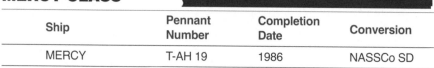

Ship	Pennant Number	Completion Date	Conversion
MERCY	T-AH 19	1986	NASSCo SD
COMFORT	T-AH 20	1987	NASSCo SD

Machinery 2 GE turbines; two boilers; one shaft **Displacement** 70,473 tonnes **Dimensions** 272.6m x 32.2m x 10m **Speed** 17.5 knots **Complement** 63 (plus 956 Naval medical staff and 258 Naval support staff).

Notes

Both ships are converted San Clemente-class super tankers. MERCY was delivered in 1986 and COMFORT in 1987. Normally, the ships are kept in a reduced operating status, one at Baltimore and the other at San Diego. The ships can be fully activated and crewed within five days. Each ship contains 12 fully-equipped operating rooms, a 1,000 bed hospital facility, digital radiological services, a medical laboratory, a pharmacy, an optometry lab, a CAT-scan and two oxygen producing plants. Each ship is equipped with a helicopter deck capable of landing large military helicopters. The ships also have side ports to take on patients at sea. Both have been fitted with a temporary hangar structure and now deploy regularly on humanitarian operations.

USNS Catawba

FLEET OCEAN TUGS
POWHATAN CLASS

Ship	Pennant Number	Completion Date	Builder
CATAWBA	T-ATF 168	1980	Marinette Marine
NAVAJO	T-ATF 169	1980	Marinette Marine
SIOUX	T-ATF 171	1981	Marinette Marine
APACHE	T-ATF 172	1981	Marinette Marine

Machinery 2 GM EMD 20-645F7B diesels driving 2 shafts; Kort nozzles; controllable pitch props; bow thruster **Displacement** 2,296.27 tonnes **Dimensions** 73.2m x 12.8m x 4.6m **Speed** 14.5 knots **Complement** 16 civilians (four naval communicators)

Notes

Fleet tugs are used to tow ships, barges and targets for gunnery exercises. They are also used as platforms for salvage and diving work, as participants in naval exercises, to conduct search and rescue missions, to aid in the clean up of oil spills and ocean accidents, and to provide fire fighting assistance. Each vessel is equipped with a 10 ton capacity crane and has a bollard pull of at least 87 tons. There are two GPH fire pumps supplying three fire monitors able to produce up to 2,200 gallons of foam per minute. Can operate as platforms for Navy divers in the recovery of downed aircraft or sunken ships.

USNS Salvor

RESCUE AND SALVAGE VESSEL
SAFEGUARD CLASS

Ship	Pennant Number	Completion Date	Builder
SAFEGUARD	T-ARS 50	1985	Petersen
GRASP	T-ARS 51	1985	Peterson
SALVOR	T-ARS 52	1986	Peterson
GRAPPLE	T-ARS 53	1985	Peterson

Machinery Four Caterpiller 399 Diesels, two shafts, 4,200 horsepower **Displacement** 3,200 tons **Dimensions** 77.7m x 15.2m x 4.7m **Speed** 15 knots **Complement** 26 (plus 4 US Navy)

Notes

Transferred to MSC in January 2006 (GRASP); July 2006 (GRAPPLE); January 2007 (SALVOR) and September 2007 (SAFEGUARD). The rugged construction of these steel-hulled ships, combined with speed and endurance, make these rescue and salvage ships well-suited for rescue/salvage operations of Navy and commercial shipping throughout the world.

USNS Zeus

CABLE REPAIR SHIP

Ship	Pennant Number	Completion Date	Builder
ZEUS	T-ARC 7	1984	NASSCo SD

Machinery Diesel-electric, twin shaft, 10,200shp **Displacement** 14,384.19 tonnes **Dimensions** 153.2m x 22.3m x 7.6m **Speed** 15 knots **Complement** 54 civilians, 27 military/sponsor.

Notes

ZEUS is the first multi-mission cable ship designed and built by the US Navy from the keel up. Its two main missions are oceanographic survey and the installation and maintenance of submarine cable systems. She is fitted with a wide array of cable handling equipment including five cable tanks, cable transporters, cable tension machines, self-fleeting cable drums, overboarding sheaves and a dynamometer cable fairleader. She is also equipped with both single-beam and multi-beam (SIMRAD EM 121) sonars for bottom profiling and can deploy towed sidescan sonars and camera sleds.

MISSILE RANGE
INSTRUMENTATION SHIPS

Ship	Pennant Number	Completion Date	Builder
OBSERVATION ISLAND	T-AGM 23	1953	New York SB, Camden

Machinery Two boilers; 1 GE turbine driving one shaft; 19,250shp **Displacement** 17,288.06 tonnes (FL) **Dimensions** 171.6m x 23.2m x 7.6m **Speed** 20 knots **Complement** 66 civilians, 59 technicians

Notes

OBSERVATION ISLAND was built as a Mariner class merchant ship. She was acquired by the USN in 1956 for use as a Fleet Ballistic Missile test ship. The vessel was converted at Norfolk Naval Shipyard but placed in reserve in 1972. She was brought froward from reserve in 1977 transferring to MSC as T-AGM 23. She operates worldwide, monitoring compliance with strategic arms treaties and supporting US military weapons test programmes.

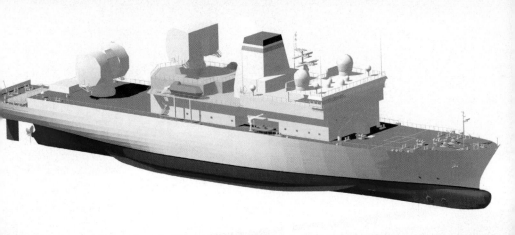

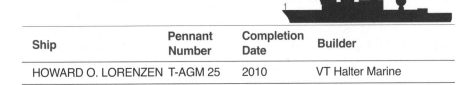

Ship	Pennant Number	Completion Date	Builder
HOWARD O. LORENZEN	T-AGM 25	2010	VT Halter Marine

Machinery Diesel-Electric; Each of four Main Diesel Generators is driven by a Cat/Mak 12M32C diesel engine; Generator sets power two main motors connected in tandem to drive a single propeller; 1 Shaft **Displacement** 12,575 tons **Dimensions** 163m x 27m x 6.4m **Speed** 20 knots **Complement** 88 mixed mariners and civilians

Notes

In 2006 VT Halter Marine Inc. was awarded a design and construction contract for a T-AGM (R) Cobra Judy replacement ship. The ship will collect ballistic missile data in support of international treaty verification using the Cobra Judy Replacement radar system being jointly developed by Raytheon and Northrop Grumman.

Construction of the ship began in 2008, and launched in 2010 with preliminary acceptance scheduled for December.

INVINCIBLE CLASS

Ship	Pennant Number	Completion Date	Builder
INVINCIBLE	T-AGM 24	1987	Tacoma Boat

Machinery Four diesel generators driving two shafts; 1,600 shp **Displacement** 2,262 tonnes (FL) **Dimensions** 68.3m x 13.1m x 4.5m **Speed** 11 knots **Complement** 18 Civilian; 18 Military

Notes

A converted Stalwart-class T-AGOS vessel, she provides a platform for a dual-band radar developed by the US Air Force to support its collection requirements against theatre ballistic missiles. She assumed her new role in 2000.

USNS Pathfinder

OCEANOGRAPHIC SURVEY SHIPS
PATHFINDER CLASS

Ship	Pennant Number	Completion Date	Builder
PATHFINDER	T-AGS 60	1994	Freide-Goldman-Halter
SUMNER	T-AGS 61	1995	Freide-Goldman-Halter
BOWDITCH	T-AGS 62	1996	Freide-Goldman-Halter
HENSON	T-AGS 63	1998	Freide-Goldman-Halter
BRUCE C. HEEZEN	T-AGS 64	2000	Freide-Goldman-Halter
MARY SEARS	T-AGS 65	2001	Freide-Goldman-Halter
NOT YET NAMED	T-AGS 66	*2013*	VT Halter Marine

Machinery Diesel-electric; 4 EMD/Baylor diesel generators; 2 GE CDF 1944 motors
Displacement 4,762 tonnes (FL) **Dimensions** 100.1m x 17.7m x 5.8m **Speed** 16 knots
Complement 25 plus 27 scientists

Notes

The contract for this class was awarded in January 1991. They are equipped with three multipurpose cranes and five winches together with a variety of oceanographic equipment including multibeam echo-sounders, towed sonars and expendable sensors. A contract for an additional vessel (T-AGS 66) was placed in Dec 2009 with VT Halter Marine. In addition to various enhancements of its equipment and electronics systems, T-AGS 66 will be stretched by 7 metres and fitted with a 5.5 x 5.5 metre moonpool for 'through hull' launch and recovery of scientific research equipment.

USNS Waters

WATERS CLASS

Ship	Pennant Number	Completion Date	Builder
WATERS	T-AGS 45	1993	NG Avondale

Machinery Diesel-electric, twin-screw; 7,400shp **Displacement** 12,403 tonnes (FL) **Dimensions** 139.3m x 21m x 6.4m **Speed** 13 knots **Complement** 32 civilians and 59 technicians

Notes

WATERS was delivered in 1993 as an oceanographic survey ship. She was converted in 1998 under the sponsorship of the Strategic Systems Programme Office. She began operations in 1999, replacing VANGUARD (deactivated in 1998) and RANGE SENTINEL (deactivated in 1997). WATERS supports submarine navigation system testing and provides ballistic missile flight test support services.

USNS JOHN McDONNELL (T-AGS 51), the last coastal surveying ship in service, was deactivated in August 2010 and delivered to the Navy Inactive Ships Programme in Pearl Harbour, Hawaii. Her shallow-water surveying capability can be undertaken by the Pathfinder class.

USNS Able

OCEAN SURVEILLANCE SHIPS

VICTORIOUS CLASS

Ship	Pennant Number	Completion Date	Builder
VICTORIOUS	T-AGOS 19	1991	McDermott Inc
ABLE	T-AGOS 20	1991	McDermott Inc
EFFECTIVE	T-AGOS 21	1993	McDermott Inc
LOYAL	T-AGOS 22	1993	McDermott Inc

Machinery Diesel-electric; 4 Caterpillar diesel generators, 2 GE motors, twin screw 1,600shp; 2 bow thrusters **Displacement** 3,396 tonnes (FL) **Dimensions** 71.5m x 28.5m x 7.6m **Speed** 16 knots **Complement** 38

Notes

Ships are built on a Small Waterplane Twin Hull, or SWATH, design for greater stability at slow speeds in high latitudes under adverse weather conditions. Ocean surveillance ships have a single mission to gather underwater acoustical data. The T-AGOS ships operate to support the anti-submarine warfare mission of the commanders of the Atlantic and Pacific Fleets. They use surveillance towed-array sensor system (SURTASS) equipment to gather undersea acoustic data. The ships also carry electronic equipment to process and transmit that data via satellite to shore stations for evaluation. ABLE was reactivated in 2008 and converted in Charleston, South Carolina to operate SURTASS low frequency active-array.

IMPECCABLE CLASS

Ship	Pennant Number	Completion Date	Builder
IMPECCABLE	T-AGOS 23	2001	Tamp SY/Halter Marine

Machinery Diesel-electric; three diesel generators; 2 Westinghouse motors driving twin screw shaft; 2 omni-thruster hydrojets **Displacement** 5,370 tonnes (FL) **Dimensions** 85.8m x 29.2m x 7.9m **Speed** 12 knots **Complement** 26 Civilian; 19 Military

Notes

The keel for IMPECCABLE was laid down on 2 February 1993. The ship was more than 60 percent complete when the shipyard encountered difficulties. The contract was sub-let to Halter Marine on 20 April 1995 to complete the ship. IMPECCABLE finally entered MSC service in October 2001. The ship has a hull form based on that of the Victorious class, but has a more powerful propulsion plant and is designed specifically for deploying an additional active towed-array system.

HIGH SPEED VESSELS

Ship	Pennant Number	Completion Date	Builder
WESTPAC EXPRESS	HSV-4676	2001	Austal Ships Pty

Machinery Four Caterpillar 3618 Diesels; Four KaMeWa Waterjets **Displacement** 750 Dwt **Dimensions** 101m x 26.65m x 4.2m **Speed** 36 knots **Complement** 12 Military, 13 Civilian

Notes

Chartered by the MSC since 2001and used for operations supporting the Third Marine Expeditionary Force (III MEF) of the USMC based at Okinawa. The vessel can rapidly transport a complete battalion of 950 marines together with up to 550 tonnes of vehicles and equipment, in one lift. Using a commercial high speed vessel to transport III MEF personnel and equipment frees about 10 military transport planes and one ship for other military purposes. Charter expected to run out in 2011, by which time the Joint High Speed Vessels should be entering service.

CHARTERED SUPPORT VESSELS

Ship	Pennant Number	Completion Date	Builder
HOS BLUEWATER		2003	Leevac Shipyards
HOS GEMSTONE		2003	Leevac Shipyards
HOS GREYSTONE		2003	Leevac Shipyards
HOS SILVERSTAR		2004	Leevac Shipyards
DOLORES CHOUEST		1978	North American SB
C-COMMANDO		1997	North American SB
C-CHAMPION		1997	North American SB

Machinery Two Caterpillar 3516B diesels driving two shafts **Displacement** 1,600 tons **Dimensions** 73.2m x 16.5m x 4.5m **Speed** 13 knots **Complement** 11 (All figures for HOS Greystone)

Notes

The MSC Special Mission Programme manages the operation of seven chartered ships used for submarine and special warfare support activities. DOLORES CHOUEST operates on the east coast and C-COMMANDO is based in Hawaii.

USNS Richard G. Mattheisen

TRANSPORT TANKERS
CHAMPION CLASS

Ship	Pennant Number	Completion Date	Builder
RICHARD G. MATTHIESEN	T-AOT 1124	1986	American SB
LAWRENCE H. GIANELLA	T-AOT 1125	1986	American SB

Machinery One Mitsubishi or one Ishikawajima-Sulzer diesel driving one shaft; 15,300shp **Displacement** 39,000 tons approx **Dimensions** 187.5m x 27.4m x 10.4m **Speed** 16 knots **Complement** 31.

Notes

This class was built for long term charter to MSC. All have double hulls and are ice-strengthened for protection against damage during missions in extreme climates. The last two are able to rig replenishment gear. All were purchased by MSC in 2003, making them US Naval Ships. SAMUEL L. COBB was transferred to MARAD in 2010; RICHARD G. MATTHIESEN will be transferred in 2011. In 2007, MSC awarded a contract to replace these vessels, which were expected to reach the end of their service lives in 2010. The first of two new chartered tankers to replace the T-5s, MT EMPIRE STATE, was delivered in October 2010 and a yet to be named second vessel, in 2011. MSC also operate the tanker MV TRANSPACIFIC on long term charter.

USNS Gordon

LARGE, MEDIUM SPEED, RO-RO SHIPS

GORDON CLASS

Ship	Pennant Number	In Service	Builder
GORDON	T-AKR 296	1996	AS Burmeister & Wan Denmark
GILLILAND	T-AKR 298	1997	AS Burmeister & Wan Denmark

Machinery Three Burmeister & Wain diesels driving three shafts; 1 x 31,400shp 2 x 23,600shp **Displacement** 57,000 tons **Dimensions** 272.6m x 32.2m x 11m **Speed** 24 knots **Complement** 45 (+ 50 USN)

Notes

Each ship can carry an entire US Army Task Force, including 58 tanks, 48 other tracked vehicles, plus more than 900 trucks and other wheeled vehicles. Two 110-ton single pedestal twin cranes make it possible to load and unload cargo where shoreside infrastructure is limited or non-existent.

• NASSCo   USNS Shughart

SHUGHART CLASS

Ship	Pennant Number	In Service	Builder
SHUGHART	T-AKR 295	1996	Odense Staal A/S Lindo Denmark
YANO	T-AKR 297	1997	Odense Staal A/S Lindo Denmark

Machinery Two Burmeister & Wain diesels driving one shaft; 47,300shp
Displacement 55,123 tonnes **Dimensions** 276.4m x 32.3m x 10.6m **Speed** 24 knots
Complement 45 (plus up to 100 USN/USMC)

Notes

Former Maersk Line container ships built in 1981 and lengthened in 1987 by Hyundai.
They were converted by NASSCo in 1993 with a stern slewing ramp, side access
hatches and improved cargo handling equipment.

USNS Seay

BOB HOPE CLASS

Ship	Pennant Number	Completion Date	Builder
BOB HOPE	T-AKR 300	1998	NG Avondale
FISHER	T-AKR 301	1999	NG Avondale
SEAY	T-AKR 302	2000	NG Avondale
MENDONCA	T-AKR 303	2000	NG Avondale
PILILAAU	T-AKR 304	2001	NG Avondale
BRITTIN	T-AKR 305	2002	NG Avondale
BENAVIDEZ	T-AKR 306	2003	NG Avondale

Machinery Four Colt Pielstick diesels driving two shafts; 65,160shp **Displacement** 62,096 tons **Dimensions** 289.6m x 32.3m x 11.2m **Speed** 24.9 knots **Complement** 27 - accommodation for 95 (plus 300 troops)

Notes

Purpose built LMSRs, rather than merchant ship conversions, these vessels have a cargo carrying capacity of more than 380,000 square feet.

USNS Dahl

WATSON CLASS

Ship	Pennant Number	Completion Date	Builder
WATSON	T-AKR 310	1998	NASSCo
SISLER	T-AKR 311	1998	NASSCo
DAHL	T-AKR 312	1999	NASSCo
RED CLOUD	T-AKR 313	2000	NASSCo
CHARLTON	T-AKR 314	2000	NASSCo
WATKINS	T-AKR 315	2001	NASSCo
POMEROY	T-AKR 316	2001	NASSCo
SODERMAN	T-AKR 317	2002	NASSCo

Machinery Two GE LM2500-30 Gas Turbines driving two shafts; 64,000shp **Displacement** 62,700 tons **Dimensions** 289.6m x 32.2m x 12.9m **Speed** 24.9 knots **Complement** 30

Notes

The largest gas turbine powered vessels afloat, they were originally to have been 36 knot ships, but costs prevented this.

SS Curtis

PREPOSITIONING SHIPS
AVIATION LOGISTICS SHIPS

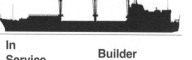

Ship	Pennant Number	In Service	Builder
CURTIS	T-AVB 3	1987	Ingalls SB
WRIGHT	T-AVB 4	1986	Ingalls SB

Machinery Two GE geared steam turbines driving one shaft; 30,000shp **Displacement** 12,409 tonnes **Dimensions** 183.5m x 27.43m x 10.36m **Speed** 23 knots **Complement** 33 (plus 300 USMC)

Notes

Primary mission is to support USMC helicopters. Additional accommodation built aft and a flight deck built forward of the derricks. Can accommodate 300 maintenance containers. Vehicles can be offloaded by a stern ramp or side door. Both ships have 10 x 30 ton cranes and a single 70 ton crane for cargo handling. Both ships are operated under contract by Crowley Liner Services. Both vessels are part of the Ready Reserve Force but are dedicated to USMC Aviation Logistics Support under the Prepositioning Programme.

MV VADM K R Wheeler

OFFSHORE PETROLEUM
DISTRIBUTION SHIP

Ship	Pennant Number	In Service	Builder
VADM K R WHEELER	T-AG 5001	2007	Edison Chouest Offshore

Machinery Two MAK V12 Diesels; 2 shafts; 16,314 hp **Displacement** 10,404 tonnes **Dimensions** 106.22m x 21.33m x 6.9m **Speed** 15 knots **Complement** 22 civilians (plus 8 USN)

Notes

Employed as an offshore pumping station capable of delivering 500,000-barrels of petroleum products from up to eight miles offshore to forces operating ashore where port facilities are inadequate or non existent, through its OPDS pipes. During an exercise in 2008 the vessel demonstrated the ability to discharge fuel over 8 miles to USNS 1st LT JACK LUMMUS and by connecting to her bulk liquid transfer system was able to pump fuel for a further 2 miles. She is assigned to Maritime Prepositioning Squadron Three and is based at Guam. SS PETERSBURG, the former OPDS delivery vessel, remains a part of the Ready Reserve Force.

MV Sgt Matej Kocak

CONTAINER & RO-RO SHIPS
SGT. MATEJ KOCAK CLASS

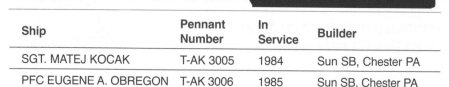

Ship	Pennant Number	In Service	Builder
SGT. MATEJ KOCAK	T-AK 3005	1984	Sun SB, Chester PA
PFC EUGENE A. OBREGON	T-AK 3006	1985	Sun SB, Chester PA
MAJ. STEPHEN W. PLESS	T-AK 3007	1985	Sun SB, Chester PA

Displacement 19,588 tons **Dimensions** 250.2m x 32.2m x 5.7m **Speed** 23 knots
Complement 85 (plus 7 MSC, 8 USN and 25 maintainers)

Notes

The second class of MPS ships chartered by MSC, they gained 157 feet amidships and a helicopter landing platform after conversion. These ships, delivered to MSC in the mid-1980s, were converted by NASSCo, San Diego, and owned and operated by Waterman Steamship Corp. Based in the Mediterranean, each ship is intended to carry 25% of the vehicles, fuel and stores required to support a USMC Marine Expeditionary Brigade. Ships have twin 50 ton and 35 ton cranes forward of the bridge and a 30 ton travelling gantry crane. T-AK 3005 and T-AK 3007 were purchased by Military Sealift Command in 2009 and their names are now prefixed by USNS.

MV 1st Lt. Jack Lummus

2ND LT. JOHN P. BOBO CLASS

Ship	Pennant Number	In Service	Builder
2nd LT. JOHN P. BOBO	T-AK-3008	1985	GD Quincy, MA
PFC. DEWAYNE T. WILLIAMS	T-AK 3009	1985	GD Quincy, MA
1st LT. BALDOMERO LOPEZ	T-AK 3010	1985	GD Quincy, MA
1st LT. JACK LUMMUS	T-AK 3011	1986	GD Quincy, MA
SGT. WILLIAM R. BUTTON	T-AK 3012	1986	GD Quincy, MA

Machinery Two Stork Werkspoor Diesels driving one shaft; 26,400shp **Displacement** 45,039 tonnes **Dimensions** 205.9m x 32.2m x 9.8m **Speed** 23 knots **Complement** 38 civilians, 10 technicians.

Notes

The 2nd LT. JOHN P. BOBO Class ships were new construction ships delivered to MSC in the mid-1980s from General Dynamics, Quincy, Mass. WILLIAMS,LOPEZ and LUM-MUS were bought by MSC in Jan 2006 for £41million ($70 m) each. T-AK 3012 was purchased by MSC in 2009 and is now prefixed USNS. The remaining vessel is owned and operated by American Overseas Marine.

1ST LT. HARRY L. MARTIN CLASS

Ship	Pennant Number	In Service	Builder
1st LT HARRY L. MARTIN	T-AK 3015	1979	Bremer Vulkan

Machinery One Bremer Vulkan MAN diesel driving one shaft; 25,700 shp **Displacement** 51,531 tonnes **Dimensions** 230m x 32.3m x 10.9m **Speed** 21.5 knots **Complement** 27 civilians, 12 military technicians.

Notes

USNS 1st LT. HARRY L. MARTIN was modified in 1999 and delivered to MSC in 2000. She is loaded with US Marine Corps equipment.

MV Gunnery Sgt. Fred W. Stockham

GUNNERY SGT. FRED W. STOCKHAM CLASS

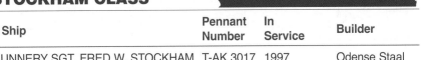

Ship	Pennant Number	In Service	Builder
GUNNERY SGT. FRED W. STOCKHAM (ex- SODERMAN)	T-AK 3017	1997	Odense Staal A/S Lindo

Machinery Two Burmeister & Wain diesels driving one shaft; 47,300shp **Displacement** 56,004 tonnes **Dimensions** 276.6m x 32.3m x 10.6m **Speed** 24 knots **Complement** 26

Notes

Built as a commercial container ship in Denmark in 1980, the ship was acquired by the Navy in the early 1990s. Following conversion to her new role at NASSCo she was commissioned into Military Sealift Command in 1997 as USNS SODERMAN. In 2000, she transferred to the Maritime Prepositioning Force, and recommissioned in 2001, being re-named GYSGT FRED W. STOCKHAM.

LANCE CPL. ROY M. WHEAT CLASS

Ship	Pennant Number	In Service	Builder
LANCE CPL. ROY M. WHEAT	T-AK 3016	2003	Chernomorskiy Zavod, Ukraine

Machinery Two Mashproyect-Zorya M25 Gas Turbines driving two shafts; 18,000shp each **Displacement** 50,570 tons **Dimensions** 263.1m x 30.01m x 10.67m **Speed** 26.5 knots **Complement** 25

Notes

Pre-positions USMC equipment at sea, enabling rapid delivery during war or contingency. One of more than 36 ships in MSC's Afloat Prepositioning Force that supports all US military services. Assigned to Maritime Prepositioning Ship Squadron One in the Mediterranean.

Capt. Steven L. Bennett

CONTAINER SHIPS

CAPT. STEVEN L. BENNETT CLASS

Ship	Pennant Number	In Service	Builder
CAPT. STEVEN L. BENNETT	T-AK 4396	1984	Samsung, SK

Machinery 1 x Sulzer diesel driving one shaft; 16,320shp **Displacement** 54,589 tonnes **Dimensions** 209.4m x 30.4m x 11.6m **Speed** 11 knots **Complement** 26 civilians.

Notes
Carries US Air Force cargo and features a climate-controlled cocoon on the weather deck to allow the ship to carry approximately 50 percent more cargo, while protecting the additional cargo from the marine environment.

MV Maj. Bernard F. Fisher

LTC CALVIN P. TITUS

Ship	Pennant Number	In Service	Builder
MAJ. BERNARD F. FISHER	T-AK 4396	1985	Odense Staal A/S Lindo

Machinery 1 x Sulzer diesel driving one shaft; 23,030shp **Displacement** 48,000 tonnes **Dimensions** 198.86m x 32.24m x 10.99m **Speed** 19 knots **Complement** 21.

Notes

Owned and operated by Sealift Inc the ship is loaded with US Air Force cargo. The ship is self-sustaining, having cranes that allow it to off-load its own cargo.

• MILITARY SEALIFT COMMAND　　　　　　　MV SSGT Edward A Carter

LTC JOHN U D PAGE

Ship	Pennant Number	In Service	Builder
LTC JOHN U D PAGE	T-AK 4443	2001	Daewoo SB
SSGT EDWARD A CARTER	T-AK 4544	2001	Daewoo SB

Machinery 1 x Sulzer diesel driving one shaft; 13,800shp **Displacement** 81,284 tonnes **Dimensions** 289.5m x 32.3m x 11.6m **Speed** 18 knots **Complement** 20 civilians.

Notes

Completed in 1985 as NEWARK BAY and OOCL INNOVATION these container ships were delivered to MSC in 2001. Both are operated by Maersk Lines and are based in the Indian Ocean as part of MPS-3 loaded with Army equipment. Charters for both vessels were extended at the end of 2005.

MV TSgt John A. Chapman

BUFFALO SOLDIER CLASS

Ship	Pennant Number	In Service	Builder
TSGT. JOHN A. CHAPMAN	T-AK 323	2002	Chantiers

Machinery Pielstick medium speed diesel driving one shaft; 23,400shp **Displacement** 41,002 tonnes **Dimensions** 204.2m x 26.5m x 10.5m **Speed** 16 knots **Complement** 19

Notes

The former MV MERLIN, she was renamed in April 2005. Another vessel with an all-weather cocoon over the upperdeck, she is loaded with US Air Force munitions and other supplies. The ship is operated by Sealift Inc. of Oyster Bay, New York.

MSC also operate the container ships MV MOHEGAN, MV AMERICAN TERN and MV VIRGINIAN on charter.

MV Pollux

READY RESERVE FORCE

FAST SEALIFT SHIPS

Ship	Pennant Number	In Service	Builder
ALGOL	T-AKR 287	1984	Rotterdamse DDM
BELLATRIX	T-AKR 288	1984	Rheinstaht NSW Emden
DENEBOLA	T-AKR 289	1985	Rotterdamse DDM
POLLUX	T-AKR 290	1986	AG Weser Bremen
ALTAIR	T-AKR 291	1985	Rheinstaht NSW Emden
REGULUS	T-AKR 292	1985	AG Weser Bremen
CAPELLA	T-AKR 293	1984	Rotterdamse DMM
ANTARES	T-AKR 294	1984	AG Weser Bremen

Machinery Two GE MST19 geared steam turbines driving two shafts; 120,00shp **Displacement** 55,355 tonnes (FL) **Dimensions** 288.4m x 32.3m x 10.6m **Speed** 33 knots **Complement** 42

Notes

The fastest cargo ships in the world, they can travel at speed of up to 33 knots and are capable of sailing from the US East Coast to Europe in just six days, and to the Persian Gulf via the Suez Canal in 18 days. Combined, all eight ships can carry nearly all the equipment needed to outfit a full Army mechanised division. All transferred to RRF in 2008.

MV Gopher State

AUXILIARY CRANE SHIPS
KEYSTONE STATE CLASS

Ship	Pennant Number	To RRF	Builder
KEYSTONE STATE	T-ACS 1	1984	NASSCo
GEM STATE	T-ACS 2	1985	NASSCo
GRAND CANYON STATE	T-ACS 3	1987	NASSCo

Displacement 16,599 tonnes **Dimensions** 203.8m x 23.2m x 5.8m **Speed** 18 knots
Complement 64

Notes
These ships are converted container ships with three twin boom pedestal cranes which can lift containers or other cargo from themselves or adjacent vessels and deposit the cargo on a pier or lighterage. Fitted with 3 twin 30 ton capacity cranes. The four forward cranes can be ganged together to lift 150 tons. Operated under contract by Pacific Gulf Marine.

GOPHER STATE CLASS

Ship	Pennant Number	To RRF	Builder
GOPHER STATE	T-ACS 4	1988	Bath Iron Works
FLICKERTAIL STATE	T-ACS 5	1988	Bath Iron Works
CORNHUSKER STATE	T-ACS 6	1988	Bath Iron Works

Displacement 26,670 tons **Dimensions** 205.7m x 24.4m x 10.3m **Speed** 18.9 knots **Complement** 52

Notes
Operated under contract by Interocean American Shipping Corporation.

ROLL ON/ROLL OFF SHIPS

ADMIRAL WM. M. CALLAGHAN CLASS

Ship	Pennant Number	In Service	Builder
ADM WM M. CALLAGHAN GTS	T-AKR 1001	1967	Sun SB & DD Co

Displacement 13,161 tonnes **Dimensions** 211.6m x 28m x 5.18m **Speed** 26 knots **Complement** 28

Notes

A ship of several 'firsts'. She was the first Ro-Ro built for the USN and initially operated under charter to MSC. She was also the first gas turbine powered vessel constructed for the USN. Originally powered by P&W FT-4s, these were replaced by the newer LM2500's in 1997. Has a capacity of 750 vehicles and 212 standard containers. Can offload using its own array of cranes (2 x 120 ton; 6 x 25 ton and 10 x 15 ton). Operated under contract by Patriot Contract Services, LLC. The ship is prefixed GTS for Gas Turbine Ship.

CAPE D CLASS

Ship	Pennant Number	To RRF	Builder
CAPE DECISION	T-AKR 5054	1985	Eriksberg
CAPE DIAMOND	T-AKR 5055	1985	Chantiers
CAPE DOMINGO	T-AKR 5053	1985	Chantiers
CAPE DOUGLAS	T-AKR 5052	1985	Eriksberg
CAPE DUCATO	T-AKR 5051	1985	Chantiers

Displacement 13,140 tons **Dimensions** 207.4m x 29.6m x 4.11m **Speed** 16 knots
Complement 27

Notes

Operated under contract by Marine Transport Lines.

CAPE E CLASS

Ship	Pennant Number	To RRF	Builder
CAPE EDMONT	T-AKR 5069	1987	Eriksberg

Displacement 12,256 tons **Dimensions** 199.1m x 28.7m x 3.8m **Speed** 16 knots
Complement 27

Notes

Operated under contract by Marine Transport Lines.

CAPE H CLASS

Ship	Pennant Number	To RRF	Builder
CAPE HENRY	T-AKR 5067	1986	Mitsubishi Heavy Ind
CAPE HORN	T-AKR 5068	1986	Kaldnes Mek Versted
CAPE HUDSON	T-AKR 5066	1986	Tangan Vaerft

Displacement 19,091 tons **Dimensions** 228.5m x 32.3m x 4.7m **Speed** 18 knots **Complement** 28

Notes

All vary slightly in design. Each ship includes a 34,000 square foot hoistable deck. Four internal vehicle decks and can carry around 1600 standard 20ft containers. Operated under contract by Pacific Gulf Marine.

CAPE I CLASS

Ship	Pennant Number	To RRF	Builder
CAPE INSCRIPTION	T-AKR 5076	1987	Bath Iron Works
CAPE INTREPID	T-AKR 11	1986	Bath Iron Works
CAPE ISABEL	T-AKR 5062	1986	Bath Iron Works
CAPE ISLAND	T-AKR 10	1993	Bath Iron Works

Displacement 14,767 tons **Dimensions** 208.7m x 31m x 5.2m **Speed** 19.8 knots **Complement** 31

Notes

Operated under contract by Crowley Liner Services Inc.

CAPE K CLASS

Ship	Pennant Number	To RRF	Builder
CAPE KENNEDY	T-AKR 5083	1995	Nippon Kokan
CAPE KNOX	T-AKR 5082	1995	Nippon Kokan

Displacement 36,450 tons **Dimensions** 212.1m x 32.3m x 10.72m **Speed** 17.6 knots **Complement** 25

Notes

Ships have two vehicle decks and can also be used to transport 1,550 standard 20ft containers. Operated under contract by Keystone Shipping Services Inc.

CAPE O CLASS

Ship	Pennant Number	To RRF	Builder
CAPE ORLANDO	T-AKR 2044	1994	Kokums AB Malmo

Displacement 12,500 tons **Dimensions** 193.63m x 28.01m x 3.94m **Speed** 17.1 knots **Complement** 25

Notes

Operated under contract by Patriot Contract Services LLC.

CAPE R CLASS

Ship	Pennant Number	To RRF	Builder
CAPE RACE	T-AKR 9960	1994	Kawasaki Heavy Ind
CAPE RAY	T-AKR 9679	1994	Kawasaki Heavy Ind
CAPE RISE	T-AKR 9678	1994	Kawasaki Heavy Ind

Displacement 32,000 tons **Dimensions** 197.52m x 32.26m x 8.5m **Speed** 17.6 knots **Complement** 29 (Full Operating Status); 9 (Reserve)

Notes

Spar decks added in 1998 to provide additional vehicle capacity. Operated under contract by Keystone Shipping Services Inc.

CAPE T CLASS

Ship	Pennant Number	To RRF	Builder
CAPE TAYLOR	T-AKR 113	1994	Sasebo Heavy Ind
CAPE TEXAS	T-AKR 112	1994	HDW Kiel
CAPE TRINITY	T-AKR 9711	1994	HDW Kiel

Displacement 9,870 tons **Dimensions** 191.29m x 27.21m x 4.05m **Speed** 16.7 knots **Complement** 27 (Full Operating Status); 9 (Reserve)

Notes

CAPE TAYLOR has a smaller cargo capacity. Operated under contract by Crowley Liner Services Inc.

CAPE V CLASS

Ship	Pennant Number	To RRF	Builder
CAPE VICTORY	T-AKR 9701	1993	Fincantieri
CAPE VINCENT	T-AKR 9666	1993	Fincantieri

Displacement 27,000 tons **Dimensions** 192m x 26.55m x 8.47m **Speed** 15 knots **Complement** 25

Notes

Spar decks added in 1998 to provide additional vehicle capacity. Operated under contract by Keystone Shipping Services Inc.

CAPE W CLASS

Ship	Pennant Number	To RRF	Builder
CAPE WASHINGTON	T-AKR 9961	1994	Stocznia, Poland
CAPE WRATH	T-AKR 9962	1994	Stocznia, Poland

Displacement 47,000 tons **Dimensions** 212.6m x 32.28m x 11.63m **Speed** 15.8 knots **Complement** 28

Notes

Former car carriers. Both have had their seven vehicle decks replaced by three stronger decks to accommodate military vehicles. Operated under contract by Crowley Liner Services Inc.

Cape Fear

LIGHTER ABOARD SHIPS

Ship	Pennant Number	To RRF	Builder
CAPE FAREWELL	T-AKR 5073	1987	Avondale SY
CAPE FLATTERY	T-AKR 5070	1987	Avondale SY

Displacement 16,490 tons **Dimensions** 272.3m x 30.56m x 4.42m **Speed** 19.8 knots **Complement** 31

Notes
Has 455 ton travelling crane to handle 89 LASH Lighters (barges) which carry pre-loaded cargo. They are floated on and off at the stern.

Ship	Pennant Number	To RRF	Builder
CAPE FEAR	T-AKR 5061	1985	Avondale SY
CAPE FLORIDA	T-AKR 5071	1987	Avondale SY

Displacement 14,230 tons **Dimensions** 249.9m x 30.5m x 4.6m **Speed** 19.8 knots **Complement** 31

Notes
Has 30 ton travelling crane to handle 77 LASH Lighters. Also equipped with two 5 ton cranes. All four ships are operated under contract by Patriot Contract Services LLC. CAPE FLORIDA and CAPE FEAR were transferred to the National Defence Reserve Force on 28 July 2006.

Cape Girardeau

BREAKBULK SHIPS

Ship	Pennant Number	To RRF	Builder
CAPE GIBSON	T-AK 5051	1988	Newport News SB & DD
CAPE GIRARDEAU	T-AK 2039	1988	Newport News SB & DD
CAPE JACOB	T-AK 5029	1986	Newport News SB & DD

Displacement 9,790 tons (8,280 JACOB) **Dimensions** 184.4m x 25.1m x 9.5m (161.1m x 23.2m x 4.7m JACOB) **Speed** 17.9 knots (17 knots JACOB) **Complement** 32-38

Notes

The term "breakbulk ships" refers to ships characterised by large open hatches and fitted with boom and winch gear or deck cranes. Commercially overtaken by containerships, they are however ideally suited for military sealift. They can be used at ports that lack their own off loading facilities. All three ships are fitted with the Modular Cargo Delivery System (MCDS) which allows them to perform standard tensioned alongside replenishment operations with US and Allied ships equipped with a dry cargo receiving station. The MCDS is a self-contained station installed on the port side forward and aft. In addition all ships are fitted with a flightdeck to allow vertical replenishment operations. CAPE JACOB is operated under contract by Matson Navigation Company. CAPE GIBSON and CAPE GIRADEAU are operated by Patriot Contract Services LLC. CAPE JACOB has been activated for duty with the Prepositioning Programme.

MV Cape Mohican

SEABEE SHIP

Ship	Pennant Number	To RRF	Builder
CAPE MAY	T-AKR 5063	1986	GD Quincy
CAPE MOHICAN	T-AKR 5065	1986	GD Quincy

Displacement 18,880 tons **Dimensions** 266.4m x 32.3m x 5.4m **Speed** 17.1 knots
Complement 34

Notes

The SEABEE is arranged much differently from the LASH configured vessels in that it has three decks on which the cargo barges or container flats are stowed. Barges are brought to each deck level by a stern elevator and are moved internally within the ship by the Transporter (conveyor) System. Two barges can be loaded or discharged in about 40 minutes. These ships have a capacity of 38 barges. Operated under Contract by Ocean Duchess Inc.

USN & USMC AVIATION

US Naval Aviation is one of the world's most powerful air forces, operating around 3,800 aircraft. Operating 11 aircraft carriers and 10 'flat-top' Amphibious vessels, the aircraft of the USN and USMC are able to project power from the sea, deep inland, with the USMC traditionally concentrating on providing troops ashore with close air support and amphibious airlift.

The USN operate ten Carrier Air Wings (CVW) each comprising fixed wing aircraft squadrons capable of undertaking most warfare roles, fighter, strike, electronic warfare, airborne early warning, sea control and aerial refuelling. In addition two helicopter squadrons are also operated. There is usually a fixed wing logistic detachment of two aircraft embarked for cargo, mail and personnel transfer between ship and shore.

A typical CVW is likely to include four squadrons of F/A-18 Hornet (48 aircraft), four EA-6B Prowlers/EA-18G Growlers, four E-2C Hawkeye and two C-2A Greyhound aircraft. The two helicopter squadrons (20 aircraft) are spread throughout ships of the Carrier Strike Group.

The USN also maintains a significant force of land-based aircraft for both frontline and support roles. The traditional submarine hunting and maritime surveillance roles of the P-3 Orion has been augmented in recent years giving the aircraft a potent strike capability, though these ageing aircraft are soon to be replaced by the P-8A Poseidon.

USN and USMC aviation is going through quite a transition in terms of both aircraft and organisation. The venerable F-14 Tomcat has now paid off from service, to be replaced by the F/A-18 Super Hornet. The S-3B has now been withdrawn from operational service, the ASW role having been taken over by the MH-60 helicopter and its tanking role eventually being adopted by the F/A-18. Another aircraft in the twilight of its career is the EA-6B Prowler, being gradually replaced by the EA-18 Growler. The USMC is seeing increasing numbers of the MV-22 Osprey Tilt-rotor enter service, while its venerable Huey and Cobra helicopters are being replaced by newer and upgraded variants, with a similar programme underway for the CH-53 Sea Stallion. The most significant change however, over the next few years, will be the introduction of the F-35 Lightning to both services. This fifth generation stealth jet will replace much of the current 'at sea' fast jet fleet if budget and production issues can be sorted.

More and more relevant to operations today is the introduction of Unmanned Aerial Vehicles. Both the USN and USMC operate ever more sophisticated UAVs and development is now looking at totally autonomous aircraft which will launch and recover from a flight deck without a pilot. Progress with such projects is so rapid that there is the possibility that it might overtake the development of the F-35 programme, and therefore have an impact on the final numbers of F-35s being acquired.

AIRCRAFT OF THE UNITED STATES NAVY
Squadron Numbers

Squadron	Nickname	Squadron	Nickname
FA-18 Super Hornet		VFA-131	WILDCATS
		VFA-146	BLUE DIAMONDS
VFA-2	BOUNTY HUNTERS	VFA-151	FIGHTING VIGILANTES
VFA-11	RED RIPPERS	VFA-192	GOLDEN DRAGONS
VFA-14	TOPHATTERS	VFA-195	DAMBUSTERS
VFA-22	FIGHTING REDCOCKS	VFA-204(R)	RIVER RATTLERS
VFA-27	ROYAL MACES	VFC-12(R)	FIGHTING OMARS
VFA-31	TOMCATTERS		
VFA-32	SWORDSMEN	**EA-18G Growler**	
VFA-41	BLACK ACES		
VFA-81	SUNLINERS	VAQ-129	VIKINGS
VFA-102	DIAMONDBACKS	VAQ-132	SCORPIONS
VFA-103	JOLLY ROGERS	VAQ-138	YELLOWJACKETS
VFA-105	GUNSLINGERS	VAQ-141	SHADOWHAWKS
VFA-115	EAGLES		
VFA-122	FLYING EAGLES	**EA-6B Prowler**	
VFA-136	KNIGHTHAWKS		
VFA-137	KESTRELS	VAQ-130	ZAPPERS
VFA-143	PUKING DOGS	VAQ-131	LANCERS
VFA-147	ARGONAUTS	VAQ-133	WIZARDS
VFA-154	BLACK KNIGHTS	VAQ-134	GARUDAS
VFA-211	FLYING CHECKMATES	VAQ-135	BLACK RAVENS
VFA-213	BLACK LIONS	VAQ-136	GAUNTLETS
		VAQ-137	ROOKS
FA-18 Hornet		VAQ-139	COUGARS
		VAQ-140	PATRIOTS
VFA-15	VALIONS	VAQ-142	GRAY WOLVES
VFA-25	FIST OF THE FLEET	VAQ-209	STAR WARRIORS
VFA-34	BLUE BLASTERS		
VFA-37	BULLS	**E-2C Hawkeye**	
VFA-83	RAMPAGERS		
VFA-86	SIDEWINDERS	VAW-77(R)	NIGHT WOLVES
VFA-87	GOLDEN WARRIORS	VAW-112	GOLDEN HAWKS
VFA-94	MIGHTY SHRIKES	VAW-113	BLACK EAGLES
VFA-97	WARHAWKS	VAW-115	LIBERTY BELLS
VFA-106	GLADIATORS	VAW-116	SUN KINGS
VFA-113	STINGERS	VAW-117	WALLBANGERS
VFA-125	ROUGH RAIDERS	VAW-120	GREYHAWKS

Squadron	Nickname	Squadron	Nickname
VAW-121	BLUETAILS	VR-54 (R)	REVELERS
VAW-123	SCREWTOPS	VR-55 (R)	MINUTEMEN
VAW-124	BEAR ACES	VR-62 (R)	NOMADS
VAW-125	TIGERTAILS	VR-64 (R)	THE CONDORS
VAW-126	SEAHAWKS		

C-2A Greyhound

C-9B Skytrain

VRC-30	PROVIDERS	VR-46(R)	EAGLES
VRC-40	RAWHIDES	VR-52(R)	TASK MASTERS
		VR-56(R)	GLOBE MASTERS
		VR-61(R)	ISLANDERS

E-6B Mercury

C-40A Clipper

VQ-3	IRONMAN		
VQ-4	SHADOWS	VR-57	CONQUISTADORS
VQ-7	ROUGHNECKS	VR-58	SUNSEEKERS
		VR-59	LONE STAR EXPRESS

P-3/EP-3 Orion

C-20A/D/G and C-37 Gulfstream

VP-1	SCREAMING EAGLES	VR-1(R)	STARLIFTERS
VP-4	SKINNY DRAGONS	VR-48(R)	SKYLINERS
VP-5	MAD FOXES	VR-51(R)	WINDJAMMERS
VP-8	TIGERS		
VP-9	GOLDEN EAGLES		

SH-60F/HH-60H Seahawk

VP-10	RED LANCERS		
VP-16	WAR EAGLES	HS-4	BLACK KNIGHTS
VP-26	TRIDENTS	HS-5	NIGHTDIPPERS
VP-30	PRO'S NEST	HS-6	INDIANS
VP-40	FIGHTING MARLINS	HS-7	DUSTY DOGS
VP-45	PELICANS	HS-10	WAR HAWKS
VP-46	GREY KNIGHTS	HS-11	DRAGONSLAYERS
VP-47	GOLDEN SWORDSMEN	HS-14	CHARGERS
VP-62(R)	BROAD ARROWS	HS-15	RED LIONS
VP-69(R)	TOTEMS	HSC-84 (R)	RED WOLVES
VQ-1	WORLD WATCHERS		
VQ-2	BATMEN		
VPU-1	OLD BUZZARDS	**SH-60B/MH-60R Seahawk**	
VPU-2	WIZARDS		

C-130 Hercules

		HSL-37	EASY RIDERS
		HSL-40	AIRWOLVES
		HSL-42	PROUD WARRIORS
VR-53 (R)	CAPITAL EXPRESS	HSL-43	BATTLE CATS

Squadron	Nickname	Squadron	Nickname
HSL-45	WOLFPACK	VT-28	RANGERS
HSL-46	GRANDMASTERS		
HSL-48	VIPERS	**T-45 Goshawk**	
HSL-49	SCORPIONS		
HSL-51	WARLORDS	VT-7	EAGLES
HSL-60(R)	JAGUARS	VT-9	TIGERS
HSM-41	SEAHAWKS	VT-21	REDHAWKS
HSM-70	SPARTANS	VT-22	GOLDEN EAGLES
HSM-71	RAPTORS		
HSM-74	SWAMP FOX	**T-6A Texan II**	
HSM-77	SABERHAWKS		
		VT-3	RED KNIGHTS
MH-60S Knighthawk		VT-4	WARBUCKS
		VT-10	WILDCATS
HSC-2	FLEET ANGELS		
HSC-3	MERLINS	**T-44 Pegasus**	
HSC-8	EIGHT-BALLERS		
HSC-9	TRIDENTS	VT-31	WISE OWLS
HSC-12	GOLDEN FALCONS		
HSC-21	BLACKJACKS	**TC-12 Huron**	
HSC-22	SEA KNIGHTS		
HSC-23	WILDCARDS	VT-35	STINGRAYS
HSC-25	ISLAND KNIGHTS		
HSC-26	CHARGERS	**TH-57 Sea Ranger**	
HSC-28	DRAGON WHALES		
HSC-85	HIGH ROLERS	HT-8	EIGHTBALLERS
		HT-18	VIGILANT EAGLES
MH-53E Sea Dragon		HT-28	HELIONS
HM-14(R)	VANGUARD	**F-5F/N Aggressors**	
HM-15(R)	BLACKHAWKS		
		VFC-13	SAINTS
T-39 Sabreliner		VFC-111	SUNDOWNERS
VT-86	SABREHAWKS	**Operational Test & Evaluation**	
T-34C Turbo Mentor		VX-1	PIONEERS
		VX-9	VAMPIRES
VT-2	DOER BIRDS	VX-20	FORCE
VT-6	SHOOTERS	HX-21	BLACKJACK
VT-27	BOOMERS	VX-23	SALTY DOGS

Squadron Nickname	Squadron Nickname
VX-30 BLOODHOUNDS	VX-31 DUST DEVILS

AIRCRAFT OF THE US MARINE CORPS
Squadron Numbers

Marine Corps aviation is organised differently to the USN. There are four Marine Air Wings (MAW) and within each MAW there are three to four Marine Air Groups (MAG). Each MAG can be assigned any number of squadrons, each with differing roles and aircraft. In some cases aircraft can be drawn from individual squadrons and assigned to a composite squadron - so for example it is not unusual to see fixed wing Harrier aircraft assigned to a Heavy Lift Helicopter squadron. To make this section easier to read, where more than one type of aircraft is commonly assigned to a squadron, I have listed those squadrons by role, rather than aircraft type.

Squadron Nickname	Squadron Nickname
FA-18 Hornet (All Weather)	VMA-223 BULLDOGS
	VMA-231 ACE OF SPADES
VMFA(AW)-121 GREEN KNIGHTS	VMA-311 TOMCATS
VMFA(AW)-224 BENGALS	VMA-513 FLYING NIGHTMARES
VMFA(AW)-225 VIKINGS	VMA-542 TIGERS
VMFA(AW)-242 BATS	VMAT-203 HAWKS
VMFA(AW)-533 HAWKS	
	F-35B Lightning
FA-18 Hornet	
	VMFAT-501 WARLORDS
VMFA-112 COWBOYS	
VMFA-115 SILVER EAGLES	**EA-6B Prowler**
VMFA-122 WEREWOLVES	
VMFA-232 RED DEVILS	VMAQ-1 BANSHEES
VMFA-251 THUNDERBOLTS	VMAQ-2 DEATH JESTERS
VMFA-312 CHECKERBOARDS	VMAQ-3 MOON DOGS
VMFA-314 BLACK KNIGHTS	VMAQ-4 SEAHAWKS
VMFA-323 DEATH RATTLERS	
VMFAT-101 SHARPSHOOTERS	**V-22 Osprey**
	VMM-161 GRAYHAWKS
AV-8 Harrier	VMM-162 GOLDEN EAGLES
	VMM-166 SEA ELKS
VMA-211 AVENGERS	VMM-261 RAGING BULLS
VMA-214 BLACK SHEEP	

Squadron	Nickname	Squadron	Nickname
VMM-263	THUNDER EAGLES	HMLA-169	VIPERS
VMM-264	BLACK KNIGHTS	HMLA-267	BLACK ACES
VMM-266	FIGHTING GRIFFINS	HMLA-269	GUN RUNNERS
VMM-365	BLUE KNIGHTS	HMLA-367	SCARFACES
VMMT-204	RAPTORS	HMLA-369	GUNFIGHTERS
		HMLA-467	SABERS
Heavy Helicopter		HMLA-469	VENGEANCE
		HMLA-773	COBRAS
HMH-361	FLYING TIGERS	HMLAT-303	ATLAS
HMH-362	UGLY ANGELS		
HMH-363	RED LIONS	**Unmanned Aerial Vehicles**	
HMH-366	HAMMERHEADS		
HMH-461	IRON HORSES	VMU-1	WATCHDOGS
HMH-462	HEAVY HAULERS	VMU-2	NIGHT OWLS
HMH-463	PEGASUS	VMU-3	PHANTOMS
HMH-464	CONDORS		
HMH-465	WAR HORSES	**Tanker and Transport**	
HMH-466	WOLFPACK		
HMH-772	HUSTLERS	VMGR-152	SUMOS
HMT-302	PHOENIX	VMGR-234	RANGERS
		VMGR-252	OTIS
Medium Helicopter		VMGR-352	RAIDERS
		VMGR-452	YANKEES
HMM-163	RIDGE RUNNERS		
HMM-165	WHITE KNIGHTS	**Dissimilar Air Combat**	
HMM-262	FLYING TIGERS		
HMM-265	DRAGONS	VMFT-401	SNIPERS
HMM-268	RED DRAGONS		
HMM-364	PURPLE FOXES	**VIP Transport/Operational Test**	
HMM-764	MOONLIGHT		
HMM-774	WILD GOOSE	HMX-1	KNIGHTHAWKS
HMMT-164	KNIGHT RIDERS	VMR-1	ROADRUNNERS
		VMX-22	ARGONAUTS
Light/Attack Helicopter			
HMLA-167	WARRIORS		

Lockheed F-35 LIGHTNING II

Variants F-35B; F-35C
Role Multi-role attack and fighter aircraft
Engines Single Pratt & Whitney F135 turbofan engine. 43,000 pounds max (in addition a Rolls-Royce/Allison shaft-driven lift-fan in F-35B)
Length 15.4 metres (F-35B); 15.5 metres (F-35C) **Height** 4.6 metres (F-35B); 4.7 metres (F-35C) **Wingspan** 10.7 metres (F-35B); 13.1 metres (F-35C)
Weight Maximum Take Off Gross Weight 22,680 kg
Speed Mach 1.6 **Ceiling** 50,000+ feet
Range 450-600 nm.
Crew One
Armament One external 25-mm GAU-12 gun pod; four hardpoints in two internal weapon bays plus six external hardpoints for a mix of missiles and precision guided bombs

Notes

The F-35 is intended to be the future of USN/USMC fast jet strike aircraft. It is a fifth-generation, single-seat, single-engine stealth multi-role fighter that is designed to conduct close air support, tactical bombing, and air defence missions. The F-35B is a Vertical/Short Take-off and Landing variant being acquired for the USMC, while the F-35C is a carrier based variant for the USN with a larger wing area and optimised for catapult take-off and arrested landings.

Four F-35Bs are undergoing testing at NAS Patuxent River. The USMC stood up the first of three Fleet Readiness Squadrons in April 2010 when VMFAT-501 was activated. The first operational squadron of F-35Bs is expected to stand up in 2012 while the F-35C will follow in 2014. They will eventually replace FA-18, AV-8 and EA-6B aircraft in service.

Boeing F/A-18 SUPER HORNET

Variants F/A-18E; F/A-18F

Role Multi-role attack and fighter aircraft

Engines Two F414-GE-400 turbofan engines. 22,000 pounds (9,977 kg) static thrust per engine.

Length 18.5 metres **Height** 4.87 metres **Wingspan** 13.68 metres

Weight Maximum Take Off Gross Weight 29,932 kg

Speed Mach 1.8+ **Ceiling** 50,000+ feet

Range Combat - 1,275 nautical miles, clean plus two AIM-9s; Ferry - 1,660 nautical miles, two AIM-9s, three 480 gallon tanks retained.

Crew E model: One; F model: Two.

Armament One M61A1/A2 Vulcan 20mm cannon; AIM 9 Sidewinder, AIM-9X (projected), AIM 7 Sparrow, AIM-120 AMRAAM, Harpoon, Harm, SLAM, SLAM-ER (projected), Maverick missiles; Joint Stand-Off Weapon (JSOW); Joint Direct Attack Munition (JDAM); Data Link Pod; Paveway Laser Guided Bomb; various general purpose bombs, mines and rockets

Notes

The F/A-18E/F provides the carrier strike group with a strike fighter that has significant growth potential and increased range, endurance and ordnance-carrying capabilities over its predecessors. The F/A-18E/F has replaced the F-14 and early model F/A-18s. Pacific Fleet aircraft are based at NAS Lemoore, California. The first Super Hornet squadron was forward deployed to NAF Atsugi, Japan in November 2003. NAS Oceana, Virginia and MCAS Cherry Point, North Carolina are the Atlantic Fleet home bases. 432 aircraft were scheduled to be delivered by 2009. A contract awarded in September 2010 will see the acquisition of a further 66 aircraft for delivery from 2012 to 2015.

Boeing F/A-18 HORNET

Variants F/A-18A; F/A-18B; F/A-18C; F/A-18D
Role All-weather attack and fighter aircraft
Engines Two F404-GE-400 turbofan engines. 16,000 pounds static thrust each.
Length 17.06 metres **Height** 4.87 metres **Wingspan** 11.43 metres
Speed Mach 1.8+. **Ceiling** 50,000+ feet
Range Fighter mission - 400 nautical miles; Attack mission - 575 nautical miles; Ferry - 2,000 nautical miles.
Crew A/C model: One; B/D model: Two.
Armament One M61A1/A2 Vulcan 20mm cannon; AIM 9 Sidewinder, AIM-9X (projected), AIM 7 Sparrow, AIM-120 AMRAAM, Harpoon, Harm, SLAM, SLAM-ER (projected), Maverick missiles; Joint Stand-Off Weapon (JSOW); Joint Direct Attack Munition (JDAM); Data Link Pod; Paveway Laser Guided Bomb; various general purpose bombs, mines and rockets

Notes

The F/A-18 Hornet is Naval Aviation's principal strike-fighter. This state-of-the-art, multi-mission aircraft serves in both the USN and Marine Corps. Although the F/A-18A to D are out of production, the existing inventory of approximately 681 Navy and Marine Corps aircraft will continue to comprise half of Naval Aviation's strike assets through 2012, and will continue to serve in active squadrons until 2023.

There are 30 Active USN squadrons and three reserve. The USMC operate 168 aircraft in 10 active and four reserve squadrons.

Grumman E-2 HAWKEYE

Variants E-2C, E-2D
Role Airborne Command & Control, Battle Space Management
Engines Two Allison T-56-A427 turboprop engines; (5,100 shaft horsepower each)
Length 17.5 metres **Height** 5.6 metres **Wingspan** 28 metres
Weight Max. gross, take-off: 53,000 lbs (23,850 kg) 40,200 lbs basic (18,090 kg)
Airspeed 300+ knots
Ceiling 30,000 feet
Crew Five (two pilots, three mission systems operators)

Notes

Usually the first aircraft to launch and the last to recover from any carrier launched mission, it provides airborne early warning and command and control functions for a battle group. Additional missions include: surface surveillance co-ordination, strike and interceptor control, search and rescue guidance and communications relay. The ten fleet squadrons fly E-2C Group II and Hawkeye 2000 variants of the aircraft. An E-2D Advanced Hawkeye is under development by Northrop Grumman. Flight testing began in 2007. The new aircraft will feature a non-rotating ALD-18 AESA radar, though it will still be housed in the circular radome. Four lots of Low Rate Initial Production (LRIP) aircraft are planned for delivery between 2011-2014 with full rate production beginning in 2013 with an objective of 75 aircraft. First deployment is scheduled for the first quarter of 2015.

Grumman EA-6 PROWLER

Variants EA-6B
Role Electronic countermeasures
Propulsion Two Pratt & Whitney J52-P408 engines (10,400 pounds thrust each).
Length 17.7 metres **Height** 4.9 metres **Wingspan** 15.9 metres
Weight Maximum Take Off Gross Weight 61,500 pounds (27,450 kg).
Airspeed 500 kts + **Ceiling** 37,600 feet
Armament ALQ-99 Tactical Jamming System; HARM missiles
Range 1,000 nautical miles+
Crew Pilot and three electronic countermeasures officers

Notes

The ALQ-00 TJS is used to provide active radar jamming support to attack aircraft, as well as ground units. Additional suppression of enemy air defences (SEAD) can be achieved through the HARM missile system. An Improved Capability (ICAP) III upgrade achieved operational capability in September 2005. This generational leap in electronic attack capability deployed for the first time in 2006. The ICAP III includes a completely redesigned receiver system (ALQ-218), new displays, and MIDS/Link-16, which will dramatically improve joint interoperability. Additionally, the ALQ-218 will also form the heart of the EA-18G Growler – the follow on platform for the EA-6B based on the Super Hornet. In addition to USN squadrons, four squadrons of EA-6B Prowlers are operated by the USMC, primarily from land bases.

Boeing EA-18G GROWLER

Variants EA-18G
Role Airborne Electronic Attack
Propulsion Two General Electric F414-GE-400 engines (44,000 pounds thrust).
Length 118.3 metres **Height** 4.9 metres **Wingspan** 13.7 metres
Weight Empty Weight 33,094 pounds (15,011 kg); Max Take-off Weight 66,000 lbs (29,964 kg); Recovery Weight 48,000 lbs (21,772 kg)
Airspeed Mach 1.8 **Ceiling** 50,000 feet
Armament ALQ-218 Tactical Receiver System; ALQ-99 Tactical Jamming System; AGM-88 HARM missiles; AIM-120 AMRAAM missile.
Range 1,275 nautical miles+
Crew Pilot and Weapon Systems Officer

Notes

The EA-18G Growler is a variant of the combat-proven F/A-18F Super Hornet Block II, and conducts the airborne electronic attack mission. It combines the capability of the combat-proven Super Hornet with the latest AEA avionics suite evolved from the Improved Capability III (ICAP III) system. The majority of the AEA-unique avionics are installed on a pallet in the gun bay and in two wingtip pods. Nine weapon stations provide flexibility for carriage of weapons, jamming pods, and other stores to meet the needs for standoff jamming, escort jamming, time critical strike, or communications countermeasures. Assembly of the first EA-18G flight test aircraft began in October 2004, and the first flight test aircraft moved into modification in late April 2005. The first production aircraft made its first flight on 10 September 2007 and was delivered to the USN two weeks later. The first production aircraft was delivered to VAQ-129 at NAS Whidbey Island on 3 June 2008, and began its initial sea trials in August. The aircraft achieved initial operational capability in September 2009. It is planned to acquire 114 aircraft to support a 10-squadron force. A contract awarded in September 2010 will see the acquisition of a further 58 aircraft for delivery from 2012 to 2015.

Boeing AV-8B HARRIER

Variants AV-8B; AV-8B II+; TAV-8B
Role Day/Night ground attack
Engine One Rolls Royce F402-RR-408 turbofan engine
Thrust 23,400 pounds
Length 14.11 metres **Wing span** 9.24 metres
Armament Mk-82 series 500lbs bombs, Mk-83 series 1000lbs bombs, GBU-12 500lbs laser guided bombs, GBU-16 1000lbs laser guided bombs, AGM-65F IR Maverick missiles, AGM-65E Laser Maverick missiles, CBU-99 cluster munitions, AIM-9M sidewinders, Litening II targeting POD to deliver GBU-12 and GBU-16 bombs with pinpoint accuracy.
Crew 1

Notes

Operated by the USMC from large amphibious flat tops or shore bases, this Vertical Take-off and Landing aircraft is developed from the original UK Harrier. The prime mission of the aircraft is close air support for ground troops. Two variants of the aircraft are in service operationally: the Night Attack and the Radar/Night Attack Harrier. The Night Attack Harrier improved upon the original AV-8B design through the incorporation of a Navigation, Forward-Looking InfraRed (NAVFLIR) sensor, a moving map, night vision goggle compatibility, and a higher performance engine. The current Radar/Night Attack Harrier, or Harrier II+, has all the improvements of the Night Attack aircraft plus the AN/APG-65 multi-mode radar. The two-seat TAV-8B trainers are undergoing an upgrade that adds new colour displays, night vision goggle-compatible lighting, and a more powerful and reliable Rolls Royce Pegasus (408) engine. The USMC operate 7 squadrons with 16 aircraft each and 1 training squadron.

Sikorsky SH-60/MH-60 SEAHAWK

Variants SH-60B; SH-60F; MH-60S; MH-60R; VH-60N
Role ASW; Anti-shipping strike; SAR; Cargo Lift
Engines Two General Electric T700-GE-700 or T700-GE-701C engines
Length 19.6 metres **Height** 3.9 to 5.1 metres **Rotor Diameter** 16.4 metres
Weight 21,000 to 23,000 pounds (9,450 to 10,350 kg)
Airspeed 180 knots maximum
Range Approx 380 nautical miles **Crew** 3 - 4

Notes

The MH-60R and MH-60S multi-mission combat helicopters deploy as companion squadrons embarked in the Navy's aircraft carriers, surface warships, and logistics ships. The MH-60R provides surface and undersea warfare support with a suite of sensors and weapons that include low frequency (dipping) sonar, electronic support measures, advanced Forward Looking Infrared, and precision air-to-surface missiles. The MH-60S provides mine warfare support and will partner the MH-60R for surface warfare missions carrying the same Forward Looking Infrared air-to-ground sensors and weapons. The MH-60S can be reconfigured to provide Combat Search and Rescue and Naval Special Warfare support in joint operations. Airborne mine countermeasures operations will be accomplished using advanced sensor and weapon packages to provide detection, localisation, and neutralisation to anti-access threats. The MH-60S will conduct the fleet logistics role in carrier strike group and expeditionary strike group operations. MH-60R/S helicopters are produced with 85 percent common components (e.g., common cockpit and dynamic components) to simplify maintenance, logistics, and training.

The MH-60R completed its Operational Evaluation in 2005 and is scheduled for a full-rate production decision in 2006. The Navy plans to acquire 254 MH-60Rs. The MH-60S was approved for full-rate production in August 2002 and is undergoing scheduled block upgrades for combat and airborne mine counter-measure missions. The Navy plans to acquire 271 MH-60S aircraft. In time these will replace the older SH-60B and SH-60F helicopters. The VH-60N is flown by Marine Helicopter Squadron One (HMX-1) and supports the executive transport mission for the President of the United States.

Boeing CH-46 SEA KNIGHT

Variants CH-46E
Role Medium lift assault helicopter
Engines Two GE-T58-16 engines
Length Rotors unfolded: 25.69 metres Rotors folded 13.89 metres
Width Rotors unfolded: 15.54 metres Rotors folded4.49 metres
Height 5.08 metres
Maximum takeoff weight 24,300 pounds (11,032 kilograms)
Range 132 nautical miles for an assault mission
Speed 145 knots **Ceiling** 10,000 feet +
Crew Normal: 4 - pilot, co-pilot, crew chief, and 1st mechanic Combat: 5 - pilot, co-pilot, crew chief, and 2 aerial gunners
Payload Combat: maximum of 14 troops with aerial gunners; Medical evacuation: 15 litters and 2 attendants; Cargo: maximum of 4,000 pound (2,270 kilograms) external load

Notes

In a Marine Medium Helicopter (HMM) squadron the Sea Knight provides all-weather, day/night, night vision goggle (NVG) assault transport of combat troops, supplies, and equipment during amphibious and subsequent operations ashore. Troop assault is the primary function and the movement of supplies and equipment is secondary. Additional tasks comprise combat and assault support for evacuation operations and other maritime special operations; over-water search and rescue support; support for mobile forward refueling and rearming points and aeromedical evacuation of casualties from the field to suitable medical facilities.

US NAVY/MCS2 KRISTOPHER WILSON

Sikorsky CH-53 SEA STALLION

Variants RH-53D; CH-53E
Role Air Assault; Heavy transport
Engines Three GE T64-GE-416 turboshaft engines producing 4380 shp each
Length 30.3 metres **Height** 8.64 metres **Rotor diameter** 24.07 metres
Speed 150 knots
Maximum takeoff weight Internal load: 69,750 pounds (31,666 kilograms) External load: 73,500 pounds (33,369 kilograms)
Range without refueling: 540 nautical miles; with aerial refueling: indefinite
Armament Two XM-218 .50 calibre machine guns
Crew 3

Notes

The heavy lift helicopter of the USMC, the CH-53E is compatible with most amphibious ships and is routinely deployed at sea. The helicopter is capable of lifting 16 tons (at sea level) and transporting the load 50 nautical miles and returning. A typical load would be a 16,000 pound M198 howitzer or a 26,000 pound Light Armoured Vehicle. The aircraft can also retrieve downed aircraft including another CH-53E. The aircraft is equipped with a refuelling probe and can be refuelled in flight giving the helicopter virtually unlimited endurance. It is to be replaced in service by a new-build derivative, the CH-53K. The CH-53K will maintain virtually the same footprint (i.e. take up a similar deck space) as the CH-53E, but will nearly double the payload to 27,000 pounds over 110 nautical miles under "hot high" ambient conditions. The CH-53K's maximum gross weight will increase to 84,700 pounds versus 73,000 pounds for the CH-53E. Up to 156 aircraft could be acquired to replace roughly an equal number of CH-53Es.

Sikorsky MH-53 SEA DRAGON

Variant MH-53E
Role Mine-countermeasures
Engines Three GE T64-GE-419 turboshaft engines (4,750 shp each)
Length Fuselage 22 metres; Overall 30.2 metres
Height 8.6 metres
Rotor Diameter 24.1 metres
Weight Max. Gross weight, w/external load: 69,750 lbs (31,693 kg); Max. Gross weight, w/internal load: 69,750 lb (31,693 kg); Empty weight 36,745 lb (16,667 kg)
Airspeed 150 knots **Ceiling** 10,000 feet.
Range Max: 1050 nautical miles.
Crew Two pilots, one to six aircrewmen
Load 55 troops or 32,000 pounds (14,512 kg) cargo

Notes

The MH-53E is heavier and has a greater fuel capacity than the Sea Stallion. Capable of transporting up to 55 troops, the MH-53E can carry a 16-ton payload 50 nautical miles, or a 10-ton payload 500 nautical miles. In its primary mission of airborne mine countermeasures, the helicopter is capable of towing a variety of mine-countermeasures systems. Aircraft assigned to HC-4 were modified with extra armour, fitted with a ramp mounted GAU-21 gun and night vision compatible cockpit lighting.

Bell UH-1 IROQUOIS

Variants UH-1N; HH-1N
Role Assault; Medevac; Utility
Engines Two Pratt and Whitney T400-CP-400 turboshaft engines; 1,250 hp
Length 17 metres **Height** 4.4 metres **Rotor Diameter** 14.6 metres rotors spread
Weight Empty: 6,000 pounds (2,721.5 kg); Max Takeoff Weight: 10,500 pounds (4,762.7 kg).
Airspeed 110 kts **Ceiling** 17,300 feet **Range** 286 miles
Armament M-240 7.62mm MG or GAU-16 .50 calibre MG or the GAU-17 7.62mm automatic gun. All three weapons systems are crew-served, and the GAU-2B/A can also be controlled by the pilot in the fixed forward firing mode. The helicopter can also carry two 7-shot or 19-shot 2.75-inch rocket pods.
Crew Pilot, co-pilot, crew chief, gunner, plus 6 to 8 combat-equipped troops

Notes

First flown in the 1950's, the venerable "Huey" still gives sterling service today. In USMC service the UH-1N can be deployed in command and control, resupply, casualty evacuation, liaison and troop transport roles. The aircraft can be equipped with a specialized communication package (ASC-26) for the command and control role and in the medical evacuation role up to six stretcher patients and one medical attendant can be accommodated. The HH-1N Iroquois helicopter is used by the USN for shore-based search and rescue duties. An upgrade programme to provide 100 UH-1Y aircraft is underway, featuring a new four-blade, composite rotor system, new transmission, undercarriage and state-of-the-art cockpit. The upgrade will provide a dramatic increase in range, speed and payload. The UH-1Y is expected to achieve full operational capability in 2012. Up to 123 aircraft are scheduled to be delivered by 2019.

Bell AH-1 SUPER COBRA

Variants AH-1W
Role Attack helicopter
Engines Two General Electric T700-GE-401 engines
Length 17.67 metres **Height** 4.17 metres **Rotor Diameter** 14.62 metres
Speed 147 knots
Maximum takeoff weight 14,750 pounds (6,696.50 kilograms)
Range 256 nautical miles
Ceiling 18,700 feet (5703.5 metres) (limited to 10,000 feet by oxygen requirements)
Armament One 20MM turreted cannon with 750 rounds; four external wing stations that can fire 2.75-inch or 5-inch rockets and a wide variety of precision guided missiles, to include TOW/Hellfire (point target/anti-armour), Sidewinder (anti-air) Sidearm (anti-radar)
Crew 2

Notes

A day/night marginal weather USMC attack helicopter the AH-1W provides en route escort for assault helicopters and their embarked forces. The AH-1W is a two-place, tandem-seat, twin-engine helicopter capable of land or sea based operations. It can provide fire support and fire support coordination to the landing force during amphibious assaults and subsequent operations ashore. The AH-1W is operated in eight composite HMLA squadrons composed of 18 AH-1 and 9 UH-1 aircraft. The AH-1W is constantly being upgraded, the latest variant including Night Targeting System/Forward Looking Infrared Radar to provide laser rangefinding/designating and camera capabilities. As with the UH-1, this helicopter is also undergoing an upgrade. 226 AH-1Z helicopters, featuring the same upgrades as the UH-1Y will reach full operational capability in 2018. The programme will achieve 84% commonality between the two aircraft types.

Northrop Grumman MQ-8B FIRE SCOUT

Variants MQ-8B
Role Unmanned Aerial Vehicle for Organic Surveillance
Engines One Rolls-Royce 250C20W heavy fuel turboshaft engine
Length 31.7 ft **Height** 9.8 ft
Weight 2,073 lbs (empty); 3,150 lbs max take-off
Load 600 pounds, including electro-optical/infra-red sensor and laser
Airspeed 110 knots   **Ceiling** 20,000 feet

Notes

Developed from the earlier RQ-8A the new model offers a significant capability increase over the first generation aircraft. The MQ-8B completed first flight in December 2006 and full low rate initial production began in 2009. By November 2009 Northrop Grumman delivered the first three production MQ-8B Fire Scout Vertical Takeoff and Landing Tactical Unmanned Air Vehicle (VTUAV) to the US Navy. Two of the three vehicles were deployed aboard the USS McINERNEY for use on a scheduled operational deployment to complete a Fire Scout Military Utility Assessment (MUA). The aircraft is designed to operate from any air-capable warship.

Both the USMC and USN operate a range of fixed-wing UAVs for a variety of missions from surveillance to strike, both at sea and overland. Aircraft in the inventory have included, Global Hawk, Pioneer and Shadow UAVs.

Bell-Boeing MV-22 OSPREY

Variants MV-22B
Role Assault transport for troops, equipment and supplies
Engines Two pivoting Rolls-Royce/Allison AE1107C engines
Rotor Diameter 11.58 metres **Blades per rotor** Three
Weight 60,500 lbs max
Airspeed 272 knots **Ceiling** 25,000 feet
Crew 3 **Capacity** 24 troops

Notes

After many years in development, this unique tilt rotor is now entering service. The Osprey completed its final operational evaluation (OPEVAL) in June 2005. The MV-22 is capable of carrying 24 combat-equipped Marines or a 10,000-pound external load, and has a strategic self-deployment capability of 2,100 nautical miles with a single aerial refuelling. It is superior to the CH-46E it replaces - twice the speed, three times the payload, and six times the range. On 28 September 2005, the Pentagon formally approved full-rate production for the Osprey. Planned production quantities include 360 aircraft for the USMC and 48 for the USN, with production at 24-48 aircraft a year. The aircraft can operate from all of the USNs big flat tops. In 2010 MV-22 aircraft deployed ashore on combat operations in Afghanistan and the first operational shipboard expeditionary deployment with a reinforced MV-22 squadron took place in 2009.

Lockheed P-3 ORION

Variants P-3C; EP-3E
Role ASW; Maritime Patrol; Recce and Intelligence collection
Engines Four Allison T-56-A-14 turboprop engines (4,900 shaft horsepower each)
Length 35.57 metres **Height** 10.27 metres **Wingspan** 30.36 metres
Weight Max gross take-off: 139,760 pounds (63,394.1 kg)
Airspeed maximum - 411 knots; cruise - 328 knots **Ceiling** 28,300 feet
Range Maximum mission range - 2,380 nautical miles; for three hours on station at 1,500 feet - 1,346 nautical miles
Crew 11 (22 EP-3E)
Armament 20,000 pounds (9 metric tons) of ordnance including: Harpoon (AGM-84D) cruise missiles, SLAM (AGM-84E) missiles, Maverick (AGM 65) air-to-ground missiles, MK-46/50 torpedoes, rockets, mines, depth bombs, and special weapons.

Notes

Originally designed as a land-based, long-range, anti-submarine warfare (ASW) patrol aircraft, the P-3C's mission has evolved to include surveillance of the battlespace, either at sea or over land. Its long range and long loiter time have proved invaluable assets. The EP-3E provides fleet and theatre commanders worldwide with near real-time tactical SIGINT. With sensitive receivers and high-gain dish antennas, the EP-3E is able to exploit a wide range of electronic emissions from deep within targeted terri-tory. A series of upgrades and inspections have been instigated to sustain the P-3C fleet as an effective force until the planned introduction of the P-8A in 2013.

Boeing P-8 POSEIDON

Variants P-8A
Role Anti-Submarine and Anti-Surface Warfare
Engines Two high-bypass turbofan engines (CFM-56)
Length 39.47 metres **Height** 12.83 metres **Wingspan** 35.72 metres
Weight Max gross take-off: 184,200 pounds (83,553 kg)
Airspeed 490 knots **Ceiling** 41,000 feet
Range Maximum mission range - 1,200 nautical miles; for four hours on station
Crew 9
Armament Five internal and six external hardpoints (four wing and two centreline mounted) all supported by digital stores management allowing for the carriage of missiles, torpedoes and mines. Sonobuoys are deployed via a rotary reloadable, pneumatically controlled launcher.

Notes

The P-8 is a military derivative of the Boeing Next-Generation 737-800. Developed as a multi-mission aircraft it will provide long-range maritime reconnaissance, ASW and anti-surface strike capabilities. The aircraft feature an open system architecture, advanced sensor and display technologies for ease of integration and upgrading.
Airworthiness-test aircraft T1 entered flight test in October 2009 and arrived at the Navy's Patuxent River facility in April 2010. T2, the primary mission-system test aircraft, arrived at Pax River in June and T3, the program's mission-system and weapon-certification aircraft completed its first test flight in July. There will be six aircraft involved in the flight test programme.
The Navy plans to purchase 117 P-8A anti-submarine warfare, anti-surface warfare, intelligence, surveillance and reconnaissance aircraft to replace its P-3 fleet. Initial operational capability is planned for 2013.

Boeing E-6 MERCURY

Variant E-6B
Role Airborne Command Post
Engines Four CFM-56-2A-2 high bypass turbofan engines
Length 45.8 metres **Height** 12.9 metres **Wingspan** 45.2 metres
Weight Max. Gross, take-off: 341,000 lbs (153,900 kg)
Airspeed Approximately 522 knots
Ceiling 40,000+ feet **Range** 6,600 nautical miles
Crew 23

Notes

The E-6 Mercury aircraft was originally designed for the TACAMO (Take Charge and Move Out) role, providing emergency command and control of fleet ballistic missile submarines. The upgraded E-6B has now expanded its role to include that of Airborne Command Post being able to take on the role of the USAF's EC-135 aircraft, thus becoming a true dual mission aircraft. The planes provide a survivable communications link between national decision makers and the USA's arsenal of strategic nuclear weapons. It enables the President of the United States and the Secretary of Defence to directly contact submarines, bombers and missile silos.

Grumman C-2 GREYHOUND

Variant C-2A
Role Carrier On-board Delivery (COD) aircraft
Engines Two Allison T56-A-425 turboprop engines; 4,600 shp each
Length 17.3 metres **Height** 5.28 metres **Wingspan** 24.56 metres
Weight Max. Gross, take-off: 57,500 lbs (26,082 kg)
Airspeed Cruise - Approximately 260 kts; Max - Approximately 343 kts
Ceiling 30,000 feet **Range** 1,300 nautical miles
Crew Four

Notes

A derivative of the E-2 Hawkeye, the Greyhound provides critical logistics support to Carrier Strike Groups. Its primary mission is the transport of high-priority cargo, mail and passengers between carriers and shore bases. It can deliver a combined payload of 10,000 pounds over a distance in excess of 1,000 nm. The interior arrangement of the cabin can readily accommodate cargo, passengers and stretcher cases. Priority cargo such as jet engines can be transported from shore to ship in a matter of hours. A cargo cage system or transport stand provides restraint for loads during launches and landings. The large aft cargo ramp/door and a powered winch allow straight-in rear cargo loading and unloading for fast turnaround. The C-2A's in-flight ramp open capability allows for the airdrop of supplies and personnel. The aircraft is currently undergoing a Service Life Extension Program (SLEP) to increase its operating service life from 15,020 landings and 10,000 flight hours to 36,000 landings and 15,000 flight hours. The changes being incorporated include structural enhancements, rewiring, improvements to the avionics and a new propeller system.

Boeing C-9 SKYTRAIN II

Variants C-9A/B/C
Role Aeromedical evacuation, C-9B cargo transport
Engines Two Pratt & Whitney JT8D-9A turbofans
Length 35.7 metres **Height** 8.2 metres **Wingspan** 27.9 metres
Weight 65,283 pounds (29,369 kg) in passenger configuration; 59,706 pounds (26,868 kg) in cargo configuration; Maximum takeoff weight is 108,000 pounds (48,600 kg)
Airspeed 565 mph at 25,000 feet with maximum takeoff weight
Ceiling 37,000 feet
Range 2,000+ miles
Crew C-9A/C, eight (pilot, copilot, flight mechanic, two flight nurses, three aeromedical technicians); C-9B, two pilots plus cabin attendants
Load 40 stretcher patients or four stretchers and 40 ambulatory patients or other combinations

Notes

The C-9 fleet is located throughout the continental United States, Europe, and Asia. The USN and USMC C-9 aircraft provide cargo and passenger transportation as well as forward deployment logistics support.

Boeing C-40 CLIPPER

Variants C-40A
Role Logistics Support
Engines Two CFM56-7 SLST turbofans
Length 33.63 metres **Height** 12.55 metres **Wingspan** 34.3 metres
Weight Maximum takeoff weight is 171,000 pounds
Airspeed 585 - 615mph **Ceiling** 41,000 feet
Range 3,000+ nm with 121 passengers or 40,000 lbs of cargo
Crew Four

Notes

The C-40A Clipper is a derivative of the Boeing 737 commercial airliner and has been procured to replace the ageing C-9B/DC-9 Skytrain II. Operated by the USN Reserve these aircraft provide critical logistics support to the USN. The USN purchased nine C-40A aircraft using a Commercial Off the Shelf (COTS) strategy, with a further two on contract. The first aircraft was delivered in April 2001.

The USN/USMC operates smaller utility logistics aircraft, including the C-12 Huron for short haul cargo transfer and VIP/Passenger transport operations.

C-20/C-37 Gufstream aircraft have been procured to operate in the executive transport role together with smaller numbers of UC-35 Cessna jets.

Lockheed C-130 HERCULES

Variants C-130T; KC-130T; KC-130J
Role Global airlift and inflight refuelling
Propulsion Four Allison T56-A-15 turboprops, each 4,300 horsepower
Length 29.3 metres   **Height** 11.4 metres   **Wingspan** 39.7 metres
Weight Maximum takeoff weight 155,000 pounds (69,750 kg)
Airspeed 374 mph at 20,000 feet
Ceiling 33,000 feet with 100,000 pounds (45,000 kg) payload
Range 2,050 nautical miles with max payload; 2,174 nautical miles with 25,000 pounds (11,250 kg) cargo; 4,522 nautical miles with no cargo
Crew Five: two pilots, navigator, flight engineer, loadmaster
Load Up to 92 troops or 64 paratroops or 74 stretcher patients or five standard freight pallets

Notes

Used by the USN in a variety of roles from transport and logistics support to launching aerial target drones. The USMC KC-130 is a multi-role, multi-mission tactical tanker/transport which provides the support required by Marine Air Ground Task Forces. This versatile aircraft provides in-flight refuelling to both tactical aircraft and helicopters as well as rapid ground refuelling when required. The latest variant of the aircraft, the KC-130J offers increases in speed, altitude, range and performance. It can be configured for cargo missions without losing the ability to conduct air refuelling, or, if the mission dictates, it can be configured exclusively for refuelling by adding an internal fuel tank. The USMC is to convert some KC-130J tankers into combination sur-veillance platforms and gunships. The renamed KC-130J 'Harvest Hawk' would retain the wing-mounted refuelling pods and tanker mission, but add a new targeting sensor and a 30mm cannon.

Boeing T-45 GOSHAWK

Variants T-45A/C
Role Training platform for Navy/Marine Corps pilots
Engine Rolls Royce F405-RR-401 turbofan engine with 5,527 pounds thrust
Length 11.98 metres   **Height** 4.11 metres   **Wingspan** 9.39 metres
Weight Take-off maximum gross, 13,500 pounds (6,075 kg); empty 9,394 pounds (4,261 kg)
Airspeed 645 mph   **Ceiling** 42,500 feet
Range 700 nautical miles (805 statute miles, 1288 km)
Crew Two (instructor and student pilot)
Armament None

Notes

Developed from the very successful British Hawk trainer, the T-45 Goshawk is a carrier-capable trainer aircraft which is gradually replacing the T-2C Buckeye and TA–4J Skyhawk as the Navy's strike trainer. The T-45A, which became operational in 1991, contains an analogue design cockpit while the new T-45C, which began delivery in December 1997, is built around a new digital "glass cockpit" design. The USN has 187 T-45s in service.

North American Rockwell T-39 SABRELINER

Variants T-39G/N
Role Twin jet and Navigation trainer
Engine Two Pratt & Whitney J-60-P-3 engines; 3,000lb thrust each
Length 13.41 metres   **Height** 4.88 metres   **Wingspan** 13.56 metres
Weight Take-off maximum gross, 18,650 pounds (8,460 kg)
Airspeed 434 mph   **Ceiling** 42,000 feet
Range 1,476 nautical miles
Crew Two (7 students/passengers)
Armament None

Notes

The handful of T-39N Sabreliners remaining in service are used to train naval flight officers in radar navigation and airborne radar-intercept procedures. These aircraft replaced the Cessna T-47A during the early 1990s. Eight T-39Gs are used for student non-radar training. The U.S. Air Force's T-1A Jayhawk is used interchangeably with the T-39 Sabreliner for advanced naval flight officer/navigator training at NAS Pensacola.

A further twin engined turbo-prop trainer, the Raytheon T-44A Pegasus (operated by VT-31 Wise Owls), is used for advanced turboprop aircraft training and for intermediate E2/C2 (carrier based turboprop radar aircraft) training at the Naval Air Station, Corpus Christi, Texas.The T-44 is equipped with deicing and anti-icing systems augmented by instrumentation and navigation equipment which allows flight under instrument and icing conditions. A number of C-12 Huron aircraft have been converted to be used in the trainer role as TC-12s (operated by VT-35 Stingrays).

US NAVY

Raytheon T-6 TEXAN II

Variants T-6A
Role All-purpose turbo-prop trainer
Propulsion one Pratt & Whitney Canada PT-6A-68 turboprop engine; 1,100 hp
Length 10.12 metres **Height** 3.29 metres **Wingspan** 10.18 metres
Weight empty, 5,000 pounds (2,268 kg.); maximum takeoff weight, 6,500 pounds (2,948.4 kg)
Airspeed 270 knots at 1,000 feet level flight
Ceiling 31,000 feet
Range 900 nautical miles
Crew Two (instructor and student pilot)

Notes

The T-6A Texan II, built by Raytheon Aircraft Company, is a derivative of the Swiss Pilatus PC-9 with a Pratt & Whitney PT-6A-68 engine, digital cockpit, Martin-Baker ejection seats, cockpit pressurisation, and an onboard oxygen-generating system. A tandem-seat, turboprop trainer, it was introduced in 2002 to train USN and USMC pilots. The aircraft is one component of the Joint Primary Aircraft Training System (JPATS) along with simulators, computer-aided academics, and a Training Integration Management System (TIMS). The USN has a total requirement for 328 aircraft by 2017.

Raytheon T-34 TURBO MENTOR

Variant T-34C
Role Training aircraft for Navy/Marine Corps pilots
Engine Model PT6A-25 turbo-prop engine (Pratt & Whitney Aircraft of Canada)
Length 9 metres **Height** 3 metres **Wingspan** 10 metres
Weight 4,425 lb, Empty Wt. approx. 3,000 lb
Airspeed Max: 280 Knots **Ceiling** 25,000 Feet **Range** Approximately 600 nautical miles
Crew Two (instructor and student pilot)

Notes

The T-34C is used to provide primary flight training for student pilots. As a secondary mission, approximately 10 percent of the aircraft provide pilot proficiency and other aircraft support services to Commander, Naval Air Force, U.S. Atlantic Fleet; Commander, Naval Air Force, U.S. Pacific Fleet; and Naval Air Systems Command's "satellite sites" operated throughout the continental United States. The T-34C was procured as a commercial-derivative aircraft certified under an FAA Type Certificate. The T-34C was derived from the civilian Beechcraft Bonanza. Throughout its life, the aircraft has been operated and commercially supported by the Navy using FAA processes, procedures and certifications.

Bell H-57 SEA RANGER

Variants TH-57B/C
Role Flying training
Engine One Allison 250-C20BJ turbofan engine
Length Fuselage - 9.44 metres; Rotors turning - 11.9 metres
Height 3.04 metres
Rotor Diameter 10.78 metres
Weight 1595 pounds (725kg) empty, 3200 pounds (1455 kg) maximum take off
Airspeed 138 mph; 117 mph cruising
Ceiling 18,900 feet
Range 368 nautical miles
Crew One pilot, four students

Notes

The TH-57 Sea Ranger is a derivative of the commercial Bell Jet Ranger 206 and is used to train several hundred student naval aviators with 45 TH-57Bs (for primary visual flight rules training) and 71 TH-57Cs (for advanced instrument flight rules training) in two helicopter training squadrons at NAS Whiting Field, Milton, Florida. Two TH-57Cs configured for RDT&E are used for photo, chase and utility missions at the Naval Air Warfare Centre Aircraft Division at Patuxent River, Maryland.

McDD TH-6B CAYUSE

Variant TH-6B
Role Training Helicopter for US Naval Test Pilots School
Engine Allison T63-A-720 turbo shaft
Length 9.33 metres **Height** 2.3 metres
Weight 2,550 lb, Empty Wt. approx. 1,138 lb
Airspeed Max: 130 Knots **Ceiling** 15,000+ Feet **Range** 300 nautical miles
Crew Two (instructor and student pilot)

Notes

The TH-6B is the Navy derivative of the MD-369H. The TH-6B is an integral part of the United States Naval Test Pilot School's test pilot training syllabus. The aircraft and associated instrumentation and avionics are used for the in-flight instruction and demonstration of flying qualities, performance and mission systems flight test techniques.

US NAVY/JO1 TRICE DENNY

Northrop Grumman F-5 TIGER

Variant F-5N (single seat); F-5F (twin seat)
Role Simulated Air-to-Air Combat Training
Engine Two J85-GE-21C turbojet engines; 5,000 pounds (2,273 kg) of thrust each
Length 14.4 metres **Height** 4.1 metres **Wingspan** 8.1 metres (figures for F-5N)
Weight 24,722 lb, Empty Wt. approx. 9,723 lb
Airspeed Max: Mach 1.64 **Ceiling** 50,000+ Feet
Range Approximately 2,314 nautical miles
Crew F-5N - One; F-5F - Two

Notes

The F-5N is a single seat, twin-engine, tactical fighter and attack aircraft providing simulated air-to-air combat training. Manufactured by Northrop Grumman Corporation the F-5F is a dual-seat version, twin-engine, tactical fighter commonly used for training and adversary combat tactics. The aircraft serves in an aggressor-training role with simulation capability of current threat aircraft in fighter combat mode. The USN also operate a number of early generation F-16A Fighting Falcons in the Aggressor role. These aircraft are primarily assigned to The Naval Strike and Air Warfare Centre (Top Gun) located at NAS Fallon, Nevada, with detachments at Key West, Florida and MCAS Yuma, Arizona. These aging aircraft will be replaced by low-houred F-5N/F acquired from the Swiss Air Force allowing the USN/USMC to operate the F-5N aircraft to 2015
.

NAVY FLIGHT DEMONSTRATION SQUADRON
THE BLUE ANGELS

At the end of World War II, Admiral Chester W. Nimitz, the Chief of Naval Operations, ordered the formation of a flight demonstration team to keep the public interested in Naval Aviation. The Blue Angels performed their first flight demonstration less than a year later in June 1946 at their home base, Naval Air Station (NAS) Jacksonville, Florida. Flying the Grumman F6F Hellcat, they were led by Lt. Cmdr. Roy "Butch" Voris. Only two months later on 25 August 1946, the Blue Angels transitioned to the Grumman F8F Bearcat and introduced the famous "diamond" formation.

Throughout the 1950s and 60s the team transitioned to various jet aircraft and built a reputation for very close, tight formation flying. In 1974 the team was re-organised into a Squadron and began flying the Skyhawk. In 1986 the team adopted the F/A-18 as its display aircraft and continues to thrill airshow crowds around the world. The six blue and gold aircraft are supported by a similarly coloured C-130T from the USMC, affectionately known as "Fat Albert". In addition to the aircraft's support and logistics role, she also takes part in the flying programme, a highlight of which is a rocket assisted take-off.

Details of the Squadrons annual display schedules can be found on their website:

www.blueangels.navy.mil

COMMAND EXCELLENCE AWARDS

The bridge wings of many USN ships proudly boast colourful displays of letters, which to the layman can be quite baffling, but to the sailors themselves are a proud display of their accomplishments. Known as Command Excellence Awards, each letter means that the ship wearing them has proven itself to be superior in specific fields of operation. The colour and letter combinations denote different departments within the ship. However, the award which most crews strive for is the Battle E. Whereas all the other awards may be awarded to all crews, there is only one Battle E awarded per squadron each year. The ship awarded the Battle E has proven itself across all departments and across all warfare disciplines. The Battle E is displayed larger than the other awards and is shadowed in appearance (see bottom right of picture below).

Awards are only valid for one year after which they must be removed, or regained. The retention of an award for a consecutive year is indicated with a diagonal strip below the letter. If the ship wins the award for five consecutive years, the letter is displayed with a star above it, replacing the stripes. In the case of the coveted Battle E, five consecutive years is displayed by a gold E with a silver star above. Further five year periods are marked by additional stars.

Sailors from the cruiser USS CHANCELLORSVILLE show off their display of awards which include a gold "Battle E". Propulsion and Engineering; Supply; Air and Maritime Warfare have all been awarded Command Excellence Awards - the Supply Department receiving the award over ten consecutive years!

COMMAND EXCELLENCE AWARDS

E   Award for the best seamanship, warfare drills, command and control, and preparedness to fulfill mission objectives. Only one award per squadron.

E   Best Propulsion and Engineering Department.

E   Best Combat Information Centre. (Surface Ships)

Award for Operations Excellence. (Submarines)

E   Best Supply Departments.

E   Maritime Warfare Excellence. (Surface Ships)

Aviation Maintenance Excellence. (Aircraft Carriers)

Best Air Department.

A   Award for Anti-submarine Warfare Excellence.

C   Excellence Award for the best Communication Departments.

CS   Award for Combat Systems Excellence on board the Aircraft Carriers.

D   Excellence Award for the best Deck Departments.

Dental Award.

DC   Excellence Award for the best Damage Control Crews.

F   Award for Fire Control Excellence.

H   Wellness Award for the best Health Promotion Activities. Units have to apply for this award.

H   Habitability Award.

or **M**   Best Medical Departments.

N or **N**   Award for Navigation Excellence.

R   Award for Repair Excellence.

T   Award for Tactical Proficiency.

W   Best Weapons Departments on board an Aircraft Carrier.

Navigation Award (Represented by a white ship's wheel)

Deck Seamanship Award (Represented by white crossed anchors).

UNITED STATES COAST GUARD

The US Coast Guard has nearly 42,000 men and women on active duty and is a unique force that carries out an array of civil and military responsibilities touching almost every facet of the US maritime environment. The USCG has roles in maritime homeland security, maritime law enforcement (MLE), search and rescue (SAR), marine environmental protection (MEP), and the maintenance of river, intracoastal and offshore aids to navigation (ATON).

The USCG was established in 1915 as a military service and as a branch of the armed forces of the USA. The USCG is unique in that it has a maritime law enforcement mission (with jurisdiction in both domestic and international waters) and a federal regulatory agency mission as part of its mission set. Until 1967, the USCG had operated as part of the Department of the Treasury but in that year transferred to the newly formed Department of Transportation. This arrangement lasted until it was placed under the Department of Homeland Security in 2002 as part of legislation designed to more efficiently protect American interests following the terrorist attacks of 11 September 2001. During peacetime and upon declaration of war or when the President directs, it operates under the authority of the Department of the Navy.

The current USCG Headquarters is at 2100 Second Street, SW, in Washington, DC. However, as part of the consolidation of Homeland Security commands, the USCG are expected to move into the new Department of Homeland Security headquarters complex which is being built on the grounds of the former St. Elizabeths Hospital in the Anacostia section of Southeast Washington, around 2014.

Since the terror attacks of 9/11 the maritime security mission of the USCG has taken on a greater importance and a programme of re-equipment and recapitalisation is underway to replace ageing vessels and introduce newer capabilities. A look at the Coast Guard Acquisition Directorate will reveal programmes to introduce the new National Security Cutter; Offshore Patrol Cutter; Fast Response Cutter and a variety of smaller vessels tasked with port and installation security. On the aviation side new fixed wing aircraft are being procured while at the same time the existing large helicopter fleet is being put through a major modernisation and upgrade programme.

SHIPS OF
THE UNITED STATES COAST GUARD
Pennant Numbers

Ship	Pennant Number	Ship	Pennant Number
Medium Security Cutter		RESOLUTE	WMEC 620
		VALIANT	WMEC 621
BERTHOLF	WMSL 750	COURAGEOUS	WMEC 622
WAESCHE	WMSL 751	STEADFAST	WMEC 623
STRATTON	WMSL 752	DAUNTLESS	WMEC 624
MUNRO	WMSL 753	VENTUROUS	WMEC 625
JAMES	WMSL 754	DEPENDABLE	WMEC 626
STONE	WMSL 755	VIGOROUS	WMEC 627
MIDGETT	WMSL 756	DURABLE	WMEC 628
KIMBALL	WMSL 757	DECISIVE	WMEC 629
		ALERT	WMEC 630
High Endurance Cutter		BEAR	WMEC 901
		TAMPA	WMEC 902
HAMILTON	WHEC 715	HARRIET LANE	WMEC 903
DALLAS	WHEC 716	NORTHLAND	WMEC 904
MELLON	WHEC 717	SPENCER	WMEC 905
CHASE	WHEC 718	SENECA	WMEC 906
BOUTWELL	WHEC 719	ESCANABA	WMEC 907
SHERMAN	WHEC 720	TAHOMA	WMEC 908
GALLATIN	WHEC 721	CAMPBELL	WMEC 909
MORGENTHAU	WHEC 722	THETIS	WMEC 910
RUSH	WHEC 723	FORWARD	WMEC 911
MUNRO	WHEC 724	LEGARE	WMEC 912
JARVIS	WHEC 725	MOHAWK	WMEC 913
MIDGETT	WHEC 726		
		Icebreakers	
Medium Endurance Cutter			
		POLAR SEA	WAGB 10
RELIANCE	WMEC 615	POLAR STAR	WAGB 11
DILIGENCE	WMEC 616	HEALY	WAGB 20
VIGILANT	WMEC 617	MACKINAW	WLBB 30
ACTIVE	WMEC 618	ALEX HALEY	WAGB 39
CONFIDENCE	WMEC 619	ACUSHNET	WAGB 167

Ship	Pennant Number	Ship	Pennant Number
Patrol Craft		SAPELO	WPB 1314
		MATINICUS	WPB 1315
ZEPHYR	WPC 8	NANTUCKET	WPB 1316
SHAMAL	WPC 13	ATTU	WPB 1317
TORNADO	WPC 14	BARANOF	WPB 1318
		CHANDELEUR	WPB 1319
Fast Response Cutter		CHINCOTEAGUE	WPB 1320
		CUSHING	WPB 1321
BERNARD C WEBBER	WPC 1001	CUTTYHUNK	WPB 1322
RICHARD ETHERIDGE	WPC 1002	DRUMMOND	WPB 1323
WILLIAM FLORES	WPC 1003	KEY LARGO	WPB 1324
ROBERT YERED	WPC 1004	METOMPKIN	WPB 1325
MARGARET NORVELL	WPC 1005	MONOMOY	WPB 1326
PAUL CLARK	WPC 1006	ORCAS	WPB 1327
CHARLES DAVID	WPC 1007	PADRE	WPB 1328
CHARLES SEXTON	WPC 1008	SITKINAK	WPB 1329
KATHLEEN MOORE	WPC 1009	TYBEE	WPB 1330
JOSEPH NAPIER	WPC 1010	WASHINGTON	WPB 1331
WILLIAM TRUMP	WPC 1011	WRANGELL	WPB 1332
ISAAC MAYO	WPC 1012	ADAK	WPB 1333
RICHARD DIXON	WPC 1013	LIBERTY	WPB 1334
HERIBERTO HERNANDEZ		ANACAPA	WPB 1335
	WPC 1014	KISKA	WPB 1336
		ASSATEAGUE	WPB 1337
Patrol Boats		GRAND ISLE	WPB 1338
		KEY BISCAYNE	WPB 1339
FARALLON	WPB 1301	JEFFERSON ISLAND	WPB 1340
MANITOU	WPB 1302	KODIAK ISLAND	WPB 1341
MATAGORDA	WPB 1303	LONG ISLAND	WPB 1342
MAUI	WPB 1304	BAINBRIDGE ISLAND	WPB 1343
MONHEGAN	WPB 1305	BLOCK ISLAND	WPB 1344
NUNIVAK	WPB 1306	STATEN ISLAND	WPB 1345
OCRACOKE	WPB 1307	ROANOKE ISLAND	WPB 1346
VASHON	WPB 1308	PEA ISLAND	WPB 1347
AQUIDNECK	WPB 1309	KNIGHT ISLAND	WPB 1348
MUSTANG	WPB 1310	GALVESTON ISLAND	WPB 1349
NAUSHON	WPB 1311	BARRACUDA	WPB 87301
SANIBEL	WPB 1312	HAMMERHEAD	WPB 87302
EDISTO	WPB 1313	MAKO	WPB 87303

Ship	Pennant Number	Ship	Pennant Number
MARLIN	WPB 87304	TERN	WPB 87343
STINGRAY	WPB 87305	HERON	WPB 87344
DORADO	WPB 87306	WAHOO	WPB 87345
OSPREY	WPB 87307	FLYING FISH	WPB 87346
CHINOOK	WPB 87308	HADDOCK	WPB 87347
ALBACORE	WPB 87309	BRANT	WPB 87348
TARPON	WPB 87310	SHEARWATER	WPB 87349
COBIA	WPB 87311	PETREL	WPB 87350
HAWKSBILL	WPB 87312	SEALION	WPB 87352
CORMORANT	WPB 87313	SKIPJACK	WPB 87353
FINBACK	WPB 87314	DOLPHIN	WPB 87354
AMBERJACK	WPB 87315	HAWK	WPB 87355
KITTIWAKE	WPB 87316	SAILFISH	WPB 87356
BLACKFIN	WPB 87317	SAWFISH	WPB 87357
BLUEFIN	WPB 87318	SWORDFISH	WPB 87358
YELLOWFIN	WPB 87319	TIGER SHARK	WPB 87359
MANTA	WPB 87320	BLUE SHARK	WPB 87360
COHO	WPB 87321	SEA HORSE	WPB 87361
KINGFISHER	WPB 87322	SEA OTTER	WPB 87362
SEAHAWK	WPB 87323	MANATEE	WPB 87363
STEELHEAD	WPB 87324	AHI	WPB 87364
BELUGA	WPB 87325	PIKE	WPB 87365
BLACKTIP	WPB 87326	TERRAPIN	WPB 87366
PELICAN	WPB 87327	SEA DRAGON	WPB 87367
RIDLEY	WPB 87328	SEA DEVIL	WPB 87368
COCHITO	WPB 87329	CROCODILE	WPB 87369
MANOWAR	WPB 87330	DIAMONDBACK	WPB 87370
MORAY	WPB 87331	REEF SHARK	WPB 87371
RAZORBILL	WPB 87332	ALLIGATOR	WPB 87372
ADELIE	WPB 87333	SEA DOG	WPB 87373
GANNET	WPB 87334	SEA FOX	WPB 87374
NARWHAL	WPB 87335		
STURGEON	WPB 87336	**Seagoing Buoy Tenders**	
SOCKEYE	WPB 87337		
IBIS	WPB 87338	JUNIPER	WLB 201
POMPANO	WPB 87339	WILLOW	WLB 202
HALIBUT	WPB 87340	KUKUI	WLB 203
BONITO	WPB 87341	ELM	WLB 204
SHRIKE	WPB 87342	WALNUT	WLB 205

Ship	Pennant Number	Ship	Pennant Number
SPAR	WLB 206	PAMLICO	WLIC 800
MAPLE	WLB 207	HUDSON	WLIC 801
ASPEN	WLB 208	KENNEBEC	WLIC 802
SYCAMORE	WLB 209	SAGINAW	WLIC 803
CYPRESS	WLB 210	ANVIL	WLIC 75301
OAK	WLB 211	HAMMER	WLIC 75302
HICKORY	WLB 212	SLEDGE	WLIC 75303
FIR	WLB 213	MALLET	WLIC 75304
HOLLYHOCK	WLB 214	VISE	WLIC 75305
SEQUOIA	WLB 215	CLAMP	WLIC 75306
ALDER	WLB 216	HATCHET	WLIC 75309
		AXE	WLIC 75310

Coastal Buoy Tenders

River Buoy Tenders

Ship	Pennant Number	Ship	Pennant Number
IDA LEWIS	WLM 551		
KATHERINE WALKER	WLM 552	OUACHITA	WLR 65501
ABBIE BURGESS	WLM 553	CIMARRON	WLR 65502
MARCUS HANNA	WLM 554	OBION	WLR 65503
JAMES RANKIN	WLM 555	SCIOTO	WLR 65504
JOSHUA APPLEYBY	WLM 556	OSAGE	WLR 65505
FRANK DREW	WLM 557	SANGAMON	WLR 65506
ANTHONY PETIT	WLM 558	WEDGE	WLR 75307
BARBARA MARBRITY	WLM 559	GASCONADE	WLR 75401
WILLIAM TATE	WLM 560	MUSKINGUM	WLR 75402
HARRY CLAIBORNE	WLM 561	WYACONDA	WLR 75403
MARIA BRAY	WLM 562	CHIPPEWA	WLR 75404
HENRY BLAKE	WLM 563	CHEYENNE	WLR 75405
GEORGE COBB	WLM 564	KICKAPOO	WLR 75406
		KANAWHA	WLR 75407

Inland Buoy Tenders

Ship	Pennant Number	Ship	Pennant Number
		PATOKA	WLR 75408
		CHENA	WLR 75409
BLUEBELL	WLI 313	KANKAKEE	WLR 75500
BUCKTHORN	WLI 642	GREENBRIER	WLR 75501
BAYBERRY	WLI 65400		
ELDERBERRY	WLI 65401		

Icebreaking Tugs

Construction Tenders Inland

Ship	Pennant Number	Ship	Pennant Number
		KATMAI BAY	WTGB 101
		BRISTOL BAY	WTGB 102
SMILAX	WLIC 315	MOBILE BAY	WTGB 103

Ship	Pennant Number	Ship	Pennant Number
BISCAYNE BAY	WTGB 104	CHOCK	WYTL 65602
NEAH BAY	WTGB 105	TACKLE	WYTL 65604
MORRO BAY	WTGB 106	BRIDLE	WYTL 65607
PENOBSCOT BAY	WTGB 107	PENDANT	WYTL 65608
THUNDER BAY	WTGB 108	SHACKLE	WYTL 65609
STURGEON BAY	WTGB 109	HAWSER	WYTL 65610
		LINE	WYTL 65611
Harbour Tugs Small		WIRE	WYTL 65612
		BOLLARD	WYTL 65614
CAPSTAN	WYTL 65601	CLEAT	WYTL 65615

USCGC Waesche

MARITIME SECURITY CUTTER (LARGE)

Ship	Pennant Number	Completion Date	Builder
BERTHOLF	750	2008	NG Ingalls Shipbuilding
WAESCHE	751	2009	NG Ingalls Shipbuilding
STRATTON	752	2011	NG Ingalls Shipbuilding
MUNRO	753	*Building*	NG Ingalls Shipbuilding
JAMES	754	*Building*	NG Ingalls Shipbuilding
STONE	755	*Building*	NG Ingalls Shipbuilding
MIDGETT	756	*Building*	NG Ingalls Shipbuilding
KIMBALL	757	*Building*	NG Ingalls Shipbuilding

Displacement 3,206 tons **Dimensions** 127.4m x 16.5m x 6.4m **Speed** 28 knots **Armament** 1 x 57mm; 1 x Vulcan Phalanx; 4 x 12.7mm MG **Complement** 106 **Aircraft** 1 x HH-65 Dolphin or 1 x HH-60J Jayhawk

Notes

This new class of cutter will be the flagship of the Coast Guard's fleet, with capabilities matched to maritime security and national defense mission requirements. The vessels have a stern ramp to accommodate small boat launch and recovery in higher sea states than conventional davit systems aboard older cutters. Each cutter is equipped with a new generation of boats, a Long Range Interceptor and a Short Range Prosecutor.

Compared to older vessels the new class have increased range and endurance (60-90 day patrol cycles); more powerful weapons; larger flight decks; chem-bio & radiological environmental hazard detection and defence; and improved Command, Control, Communications, Computers, Intelligence, Surveillance and Reconnaissance (C4ISR) equipment. The cutters are equipped with air and surface search radars and target classification sensors. The cutters' ISR range and capabilities will be extended and augmented by manned and unmanned aircraft.

USCGC Mellon

HIGH ENDURANCE CUTTER

Ship	Pennant Number	Completion Date	Builder
HAMILTON	715	1967	Avondale Shipyards
DALLAS	716	1967	Avondale Shipyards
MELLON	717	1967	Avondale Shipyards
CHASE	718	1968	Avondale Shipyards
BOUTWELL	719	1968	Avondale Shipyards
SHERMAN	720	1968	Avondale Shipyards
GALLATIN	721	1968	Avondale Shipyards
MORGENTHAU	722	1969	Avondale Shipyards
RUSH	723	1969	Avondale Shipyards
MUNRO	724	1971	Avondale Shipyards
JARVIS	725	1971	Avondale Shipyards
MIDGETT	726	1972	Avondale Shipyards

Machinery CODOG; 2 x Pratt & Whittney FT4A-6 gas turbines 36,000 hp (27,000 kW); 2 x Fairbanks-Morse 38TD8-1/8-12 12-cylinder diesel engines 7,000 hp **Displacement** 3,300 tons **Dimensions** 115.2m x 13.1m x 6.1m **Speed** 29 knots **Armament** 1 x 76mm Oto/Melara; 2 x 25mm Bushmaster; 1 x Vulcan Phalanx; 4 x 12.7mm MG **Complement** 162 **Aircraft** 1 x HH-65 Dolphin; HH-60J Jayhawk or MH-68A

Notes

They are powered by a CODOG (Combined Diesel or Gas) system consisting of two diesel engines and two gas turbines, and have controllable pitch propellers. Equipped with a helicopter flight deck, retractable hangar, and the facilities to support helicopter deployment, the youngest of these 12 cutters is nearly 40 years-old. The whole class underwent a Fleet Rehabilitation and Modernisation (FRAM) programme, from the 1980's, which included the replacement of the original 5-inch gun with a modern 76 mm Oto Melara. The primary mission of these vessels is enforcement of laws and treaties and search and rescue (SAR) on the high seas, including the US exclusive economic zone. These vessels have in recent years deployed on operations in the Persian Gulf as well as Maritime Security Operations in the Arabian Sea and Mediterreanean. These vessels are pretty close to the end of their service life (the Coast Guard's Cutter Division estimated that they could be extended through to 2012) and will slowly be replaced by the Bertholf class.

USCGC Campbell

MEDIUM ENDURANCE CUTTER
FAMOUS CLASS

Ship	Pennant Number	Completion Date	Builder
BEAR	901	1983	Tacoma Boatbuilding Co
TAMPA	902	1984	Tacoma Boatbuilding Co
HARRIET LANE	903	1984	Tacoma Boatbuilding Co
NORTHLAND	904	1984	Tacoma Boatbuilding Co
SPENCER	905	1986	Robert E Derecktor Corp
SENECA	906	1987	Robert E Derecktor Corp
ESCANABA	907	1987	Robert E Derecktor Corp
TAHOMA	908	1988	Robert E Derecktor Corp
CAMPBELL	909	1988	Robert E Derecktor Corp
THETIS	910	1989	Robert E Derecktor Corp
FORWARD	911	1990	Robert E Derecktor Corp
LEGARE	912	1990	Robert E Derecktor Corp
MOHAWK	913	1991	Robert E Derecktor Corp

Machinery Two turbo-charged ALCO V-18 diesel engines driving two shafts with controllable pitch propellers **Displacement** 1,820 tons **Dimensions** 82.3m x 11.6m x 4.2m **Speed** 19.5 knots **Armament** 1 x 76mm Oto/Melara; 2 x 12.7mm MG or 2 x 40mm Grenade Launchers **Complement** 100 (plus 5 aircrew) **Aircraft** 1 x HH-65 Dolphin; HH-60J Jayhawk; MH-68A or SH-60B.

Notes

Built in the 1980s, the ships underwent a series of upgrades which included the installation of satellite communications and upgrades to command systems. From early in the 21st century it was decided that the class would undergo a service life extension refit under the Mission Effectiveness Project. Work included upgrades to habitability and engineering spaces. TAMPA was the first to complete in 2004 and the remainder of the class will be rotated through the programme.

The Deepwater acquisition plan includes 25 Offshore Patrol Cutters (OPCs), which will replace all four classes of WMEC. The new vessels are expected to be powered by four diesel engines, with an endurance of 45 days. OPCs are to be adaptable, multi-mission vessels with a C4ISR electronics suite, and capable of sustained, intensive small boat and flight operations in support of law enforcement, defence and search & rescue missions.

The OPCs will complement the larger National Security Cutters' capabilities, including air surveillance with helicopters and unmanned air vehicles; increased situational awareness through an integrated C4ISR electronics suite; improved force protection and automated armament (including a 57mm deck gun); and improved defenses for operating in chemical, biological, or radiological contaminated environments.

A contract specification is expected to be released in the near future with delivery of the first ship planned for 2019.

• MARC PICHÉ

USCGC Alert

RELIANCE CLASS

Ship	Pennant Number	Completion Date	Builder
RELIANCE	615	1964	Todd Shipyards
DILIGENCE	616	1964	Todd Shipyards
VIGILANT	617	1964	Todd Shipyards
ACTIVE	618	1966	Christy Corporation
CONFIDENCE	619	1966	Coast Guard Yard, Baltimore
RESOLUTE	620	1966	Coast Guard Yard, Baltimore
VALIANT	621	1967	American Shipbuilding Co
STEADFAST	623	1968	American Shipbuilding Co
DAUNTLESS	624	1968	American Shipbuilding Co
VENTUROUS	625	1968	American Shipbuilding Co
DEPENDABLE	626	1968	American Shipbuilding Co
VIGOROUS	627	1969	American Shipbuilding Co
DECISIVE	629	1968	Coast Guard Yard, Baltimore
ALERT	630	1969	Coast Guard Yard, Baltimore

Machinery 2 Alco 16V-251 diesels 6,480 hp; driving 2 shafts **Displacement** 1,129 tons **Dimensions** 64.2m x 10.4m x 3.2m **Speed** 18 knots **Armament** 1 x 25mm Bushmaster; 2 x 12.7mm MG **Complement** 75 **Aircraft** 1 x HH-65 Dolphin or 1 x HH-60J Jayhawk.

Notes

Primarily assigned law enforcement and search and rescue missions the cutters usually operate within 500 nm of the coast. To aid with the SAR task the vessels have been designed with a bridge that affords 360° visibility and a flight deck able to accommodate a medium sized helicopter. Each of the cutters underwent a Major Maintenance Availability process between 1986 and 1996. Changes to the engines and generators resulted in the vessels emerging from refit with a funnel aft of the bridge. As with the Famous class cutters, a Mission Effectiveness Project was initiated for this class with DEPENDABLE being the first to undergo the upgrade work package to its living and engineering spaces in 2005. The remainder of the class will undergo similar upgrades.

Of historical interest, these vessels were originally designed to accommodate additional armament in case of national emergency. This would have comprised an additional 3-inch gun; six .50 calibre machine guns; a Hedgehog ASW weapon; two torpedo launchers and two depth charge racks. In addition they would also recieve a sonar fit.

USCGC Alex Haley

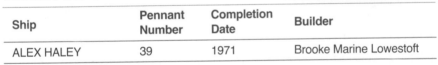

EDENTON CLASS

Ship	Pennant Number	Completion Date	Builder
ALEX HALEY	39	1971	Brooke Marine Lowestoft

Machinery Four Caterpillar 3516 DITAWJ diesels, 6,000 hp; 2 shafts **Displacement** 3,000 tons **Dimensions** 86.1m x 15.2m x 4.6m **Speed** 18 knots **Armament** 1 x 25mm Bushmaster; 2 x 12.7mm MG **Complement** 99 **Aircraft** Flightdeck for 1 x HH-65 Dolphin or 1 x HH-60J Jayhawk

Notes

The former US Navy salvage vessel USS EDENTON was recommissioned for Coast Guard duty on 10 July 1999. The stern towing machine, forward crane, and A-frame were removed and a flight-deck, retractable hangar, and air-search radar installed. She is used in the Bering Sea, Gulf of Alaska and Pacific.

• USCG/PO3 WALTER SHINN

USCGC Acushnet

DIVER CLASS

Ship	Pennant Number	Competion Date	Builder
ACUSHNET	167	1944	Basalt Rock Co

Machinery Four Fairbanks-Morse diesels, 3,000 hp; 2 shafts **Displacement** 1,745 tons full load **Dimensions** 64.9m x 12.5m x 14.6m **Speed** 14 knots **Armament** 2 x 12.7mm MG **Complement** 75.

Notes

She was originally USS SHACKLE, a Diver-class rescue and salvage ship commissioned by the US Navy for service in World War II. She underwent a major rennovation in 1983. She patrols the waters of the North Pacific and is the sole remaining World War II era ship on active duty in the US fleet.

USCGC Polar Sea

ICEBREAKERS
POLAR CLASS

Ship	Pennant Number	Completion Date	Builder
POLAR STAR	10	1976	Lockheed SB
POLAR SEA	11	1978	Lockheed SB

Machinery CODOG; diesel-electric; 6 Alco 16V-251F/ Westinghouse AC diesel generators, 21,000hp; 3 Westinghouse DC motors 18,000 hp; 3 Pratt & Whitney FT4A-12 gas turbines; 3 shafts **Displacement** 13,190 tons **Dimensions** 121.6m x 25.6m x 9.8m **Speed** 20 knots **Armament** 2 x 7.62 MG **Aircraft** 2 x HH-65A or 1 x HH-60J **Complement** 134 plus 33 scientists and 12 aircrew.

Notes

These cutters, specifically designed for open-water icebreaking, have reinforced hulls, special icebreaking bows, and a system that allows rapid shifting of ballast to increase the effectiveness of their icebreaking. These vessels conduct Arctic and Antarctic research and are the primary icebreakers which clear the channel into McMurdo Station for supply ships. All are homeported out of Seattle, Washington.

USCGC Mackinaw

MACKINAW CLASS

Ship	Pennant Number	Completion Date	Builder
MACKINAW	30	2006	Manitowoc Marine

Machinery 3 Caterpillar 3612 Turbocharged V-12 engines; 2 podded propulsors **Displacement** 3,500 tons **Dimensions** 73.1m x 17.7m x 4.8m **Speed** 15 knots **Complement** 55

Notes

Conducts heavy icebreaking to assist in keeping shipping lanes open on the Great Lakes and can be deployed from one day to six weeks. In addition to heavy icebreaking, she has state-of-the-art systems and multi-mission capabilities that include search and rescue, buoy tending, maritime homeland security operations, environmental response and law enforcement as well as the ability to deploy an oil skimming system to respond to hazardous situations. Delivered to the Coast Guard on 18 November 2005, and commissioned on 10 June 2006, she is homeported in Cheboygan, Michigan.

USCGC Healy

HEALY CLASS

Ship	Pennant Number	Completion Date	Builder
HEALY	20	1999	Avondale

Machinery Diesel-electric; 4 Westinghouse/Sulzer 12ZA 40S diesels; 42,400 hp; 4 Westinghouse alternators; 2 motors, 30,000 hp; 2 shafts; bow thruster **Displacement** 16,400 tons full load **Dimensions** 128m x 25m x 8.9m **Speed** 17 knots **Aircraft** 2 x HH-65A or 1 x HH-60J **Complement** 75 (plus 45 scientists).

Notes

The 420 foot icebreaker employs the power to break 4.5 feet of ice at three knots continuously or up to eight feet by ramming. Designed to conduct a wide range of research activities, the ship provides more than 4,200 square feet (390 m²) of scientific laboratory space, numerous electronic sensor systems, oceanographic winches, and accommodations for up to 50 scientists.

USCGC Zephyr

PATROL CRAFT
CYCLONE CLASS

Ship	Pennant Number	Completion Date	Builder
ZEPHYR	8	1994	Bollinger, Lockport
SHAMAL	13	1996	Bollinger, Lockport
TORNADO	14	2000	Bollinger, Lockport

Machinery 4 Paxman-Valenta 16RP 200M diesels, 14,400 hp; 4 shafts **Displacement** 386 tons **Dimensions** 54.6m x 7.9m x 2.4m **Speed** 35 knots **Armament** 2 x 25mm; 4 x 12.7mm MG **Complement** 27.

Notes

The remainder of five former USN vessels transferred to the USCG in 2004-05 to fill a gap for Homeland Security tasks in the wake of 9/11. Two were returned to the USN in 2009 and the remaining three will be returned in 2012.

USCGC Sentinel

SENTINEL CLASS

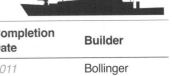

Ship	Pennant Number	Completion Date	Builder
BERNARD C WEBBER	1001	*2011*	Bollinger
RICHARD ETHERIDGE	1002	*Building*	Bollinger
WILLIAM FLORES	1003	*Building*	Bollinger
ROBERT YERED	1004	*Building*	Bollinger

Machinery Two 20-cylinder MTU diesel engines; 2 shafts **Displacement** 353 tons **Dimensions** 46.8m x 8.11m x 2.9m **Speed** 28 knots **Armament** 25mm chain gun; four .50 calibre MG **Complement** 22

Notes

The original Deepwater acquisition strategy for the FRC was accelerated by 10 years to fill the operational gap of the aging 110ft ocean going patrol boats. The award for the design and construction of the Sentinel Class Patrol Boat was to Bollinger Shipyards, Inc., on 26 September 2008 for a class of vessels based on the Damen 4708 design. The Coast Guard awarded a further $166.1 million contract option on 14 September 2010 to begin production of four more vessels, bringing the total number of FRCs under contract with Bollinger to eight with a current contract value of $410.7 million. The current FRC contract contains options for up to 34 cutters and is worth up to $1.5 billion if all options are exercised. The first Sentinel Class patrol boat will be delivered during the third quarter of 2011. It is planned to acquire up to 58 of this class. The twelth cutter should be delivered by 2013, with Bollinger anticipating delivering one vessel every eight weeks.

USCGC Aquidneck

110' ISLAND CLASS

Ship	Pennant Number	Completion Date	Builder
FARALLON	1301	1986	Bollinger, Lockport
MANITOU	1302*	1986	Bollinger, Lockport
MATAGORDA	1303*	1986	Bollinger, Lockport
MAUI	1304	1986	Bollinger, Lockport
MONHEGAN	1305*	1986	Bollinger, Lockport
NUNIVAK	1306*	1986	Bollinger, Lockport
OCRACOKE	1307	1986	Bollinger, Lockport
VASHON	1308*	1986	Bollinger, Lockport
AQUIDNECK	1309	1986	Bollinger, Lockport
MUSTANG	1310	1986	Bollinger, Lockport
NAUSHON	1311	1986	Bollinger, Lockport
SANIBEL	1312	1987	Bollinger, Lockport
EDISTO	1313	1987	Bollinger, Lockport
SAPELO	1314	1987	Bollinger, Lockport

Ship	Pennant Number	Completion Date	Builder
MATINICUS	1315	1987	Bollinger, Lockport
NANTUCKET	1316	1987	Bollinger, Lockport
ATTU	1317*	1988	Bollinger, Lockport
BARANOF	1318	1988	Bollinger, Lockport
CHANDELEUR	1319	1988	Bollinger, Lockport
CHINCOTEAGUE	1320	1988	Bollinger, Lockport
CUSHING	1321	1988	Bollinger, Lockport
CUTTYHUNK	1322	1988	Bollinger, Lockport
DRUMMOND	1323	1988	Bollinger, Lockport
KEY LARGO	1324	1988	Bollinger, Lockport
METOMPKIN	1325*	1989	Bollinger, Lockport
MONOMOY	1326	1989	Bollinger, Lockport
ORCAS	1327	1989	Bollinger, Lockport
PADRE	1328*	1989	Bollinger, Lockport
SITKINAK	1329	1989	Bollinger, Lockport
TYBEE	1330	1989	Bollinger, Lockport
WASHINGTON	1331	1989	Bollinger, Lockport
WRANGELL	1332	1989	Bollinger, Lockport
ADAK	1333	1989	Bollinger, Lockport
LIBERTY	1334	1989	Bollinger, Lockport
ANACAPA	1335	1989	Bollinger, Lockport
KISKA	1336	1989	Bollinger, Lockport
ASSATEAGUE	1337	1989	Bollinger, Lockport
GRAND ISLE	1338	1991	Bollinger, Lockport
KEY BISCAYNE	1339	1991	Bollinger, Lockport
JEFFERSON ISLAND	1340	1991	Bollinger, Lockport
KODIAK ISLAND	1341	1991	Bollinger, Lockport
LONG ISLAND	1342	1991	Bollinger, Lockport
BAINBRIDGE ISLAND	1343	1991	Bollinger, Lockport

Ship	Pennant Number	Completion Date	Builder
BLOCK ISLAND	1344	1991	Bollinger, Lockport
STATEN ISLAND	1345	1991	Bollinger, Lockport
ROANOKE ISLAND	1346	1992	Bollinger, Lockport
PEA ISLAND	1347	1992	Bollinger, Lockport
KNIGHT ISLAND	1348	1992	Bollinger, Lockport
GALVESTON ISLAND	1349	1992	Bollinger, Lockport

Machinery Two Paxman Valenta 16RP 200M diesels (C series); two Caterpillar 3516 DITA diesels (A & B series); 2 shafts **Displacement** 168 tons (A series); 154 tons (B series); 134 tons (C series) **Dimensions** 33.5m x 6.4m x 2.2m **Speed** 29 knots **Armament** 1 x 25mm; 2 x 12.7mm MG **Complement** 16

Notes

The design is based on Vosper Thornycroft UK 110-foot patrol boat. Acquired in three batches: A 1301-1316; B 1317-1337 and C 1338-1349. The initial A group were found to suffer from hull cracks and therefore additional hull plating was added in the latter two batches. Missions include provision of offshore surveillance, law enforcement, and perform search-and-rescue (SAR) operations. As such, the patrol boats were designed to have a 5-day endurance.

As a part of the Deepwater programme, a plan was adopted to stretch this class by 13 foot to accommodate a stern ramp for launch and recovery of small boats and improved C4ISR systems. The conversion was undertaken by Bollinger with the first vessel, MATAGORDA, being redelivered to the USCG in February 2004. A further three vessels were converted in 2004, with a further group of four to be converted. However, the programme was terminated after significant problems were encountered with deck cracking, hull deformation and problems with shaft alignment. All eight vessels (marked * in listings above) were withdrawn from operations in 2006, the USCG deciding that they were too dangerous to operate for their normal duties, and have remained laid up ever since.

Vessels of this class have deployed to the Persian Gulf to provide security patrols around offshore oil installations.

USCGC Shearwater

MARINE PROTECTOR CLASS

Ship	Pennant Number	Completion Date	Builder
BARRACUDA	87301	1998	Bollinger, Lockport
HAMMERHEAD	87302	1998	Bollinger, Lockport
MAKO	87303	1998	Bollinger, Lockport
MARLIN	87304	1998	Bollinger, Lockport
STINGRAY	87305	1999	Bollinger, Lockport
DORADO	87306	1999	Bollinger, Lockport
OSPREY	87307	1999	Bollinger, Lockport
CHINOOK	87308	1999	Bollinger, Lockport
ALBACORE	87309	1999	Bollinger, Lockport
TARPON	87310	1999	Bollinger, Lockport
COBIA	87311	1999	Bollinger, Lockport
HAWKSBILL	87312	1999	Bollinger, Lockport
CORMORANT	87313	1999	Bollinger, Lockport
FINBACK	87314	1999	Bollinger, Lockport
AMBERJACK	87315	1999	Bollinger, Lockport

Ship	Pennant Number	Completion Date	Builder
KITTIWAKE	87316	2000	Bollinger, Lockport
BLACKFIN	87317	2000	Bollinger, Lockport
BLUEFIN	87318	2000	Bollinger, Lockport
YELLOWFIN	87319	2000	Bollinger, Lockport
MANTA	87320	2000	Bollinger, Lockport
COHO	87321	2000	Bollinger, Lockport
KINGFISHER	87322	2000	Bollinger, Lockport
SEAHAWK	87323	2000	Bollinger, Lockport
STEELHEAD	87324	2000	Bollinger, Lockport
BELUGA	87325	2000	Bollinger, Lockport
BLACKTIP	87326	2000	Bollinger, Lockport
PELICAN	87327	2000	Bollinger, Lockport
RIDLEY	87328	2000	Bollinger, Lockport
COCHITO	87329	2001	Bollinger, Lockport
MANOWAR	87330	2001	Bollinger, Lockport
MORAY	87331	2001	Bollinger, Lockport
RAZORBILL	87332	2001	Bollinger, Lockport
ADELIE	87333	2001	Bollinger, Lockport
GANNET	87334	2001	Bollinger, Lockport
NARWHAL	87335	2001	Bollinger, Lockport
STURGEON	87336	2001	Bollinger, Lockport
SOCKEYE	87337	2001	Bollinger, Lockport
IBIS	87338	2001	Bollinger, Lockport
POMPANO	87339	2001	Bollinger, Lockport
HALIBUT	87340	2001	Bollinger, Lockport
BONITO	87341	2001	Bollinger, Lockport
SHRIKE	87342	2002	Bollinger, Lockport
TERN	87343	2002	Bollinger, Lockport
HERON	87344	2002	Bollinger, Lockport
WAHOO	87345	2002	Bollinger, Lockport

Ship	Pennant Number	Completion Date	Builder
FLYING FISH	87346	2002	Bollinger, Lockport
HADDOCK	87347	2002	Bollinger, Lockport
BRANT	87348	2002	Bollinger, Lockport
SHEARWATER	87349	2002	Bollinger, Lockport
PETREL	87350	2002	Bollinger, Lockport
SEALION	87352	2003	Bollinger, Lockport
SKIPJACK	87353	2003	Bollinger, Lockport
DOLPHIN	87354	2004	Bollinger, Lockport
HAWK	87355	2004	Bollinger, Lockport
SAILFISH	87356	2004	Bollinger, Lockport
SAWFISH	87357	2004	Bollinger, Lockport
SWORDFISH	87358	2005	Bollinger, Lockport
TIGER SHARK	87359	2005	Bollinger, Lockport
BLUE SHARK	87360	2005	Bollinger, Lockport
SEA HORSE	87361	2005	Bollinger, Lockport
SEA OTTER	87362	2005	Bollinger, Lockport
MANATEE	87363	2005	Bollinger, Lockport
AHI	87364	2006	Bollinger, Lockport
PIKE	87365	2006	Bollinger, Lockport
TERRAPIN	87366	2006	Bollinger, Lockport
SEA DRAGON	87367	2008	Bollinger, Lockport
SEA DEVIL	87368	2008	Bollinger, Lockport
CROCODILE	87369	2008	Bollinger, Lockport
DIAMONDBACK	87370	2008	Bollinger, Lockport
REEF SHARK	87371	2008	Bollinger, Lockport
ALLIGATOR	87372	2009	Bollinger, Lockport
SEA DOG	87373	2009	Bollinger, Lockport
SEA FOX	87374	2009	Bollinger, Lockport

Machinery Two MTU 8V 396TE94 diesels; 2 shafts **Displacement** 91 tons **Dimensions** 26.5m x 5.8m x 1.6m **Speed** 25 knots **Armament** 2 x 12.7mm MG **Complement** 10

Notes

The 87' Coastal Patrol Boat was tailored to meet a myriad of Coast Guard missions, including Search and Rescue, Law Enforcement, Fisheries, Drug Interdiction, and Alien Interdiction. This class has also proven to be versatile in adapting to Homeland Security missions.

SEA DRAGON, SEA DEVIL, SEA DOG and SEA FOX were paid for by the US Navy and manned by the Coast Guard. They are used to escort USN submarines (principally the Ohio Class Trident missile carrying submarines) in and out of port at Bangor and Kings Bay (SEA DRAGON & SEA DOG at King's Bay, the other pair at Bangor). All four are fitted with a remote controlled 50-cal mount on a raised platform on the forecastle, in addition to the regular crew served 50's. A FLIR sight is mounted on the mast and a joystick control is in the pilot house with a TV monitor, etc. The mount was first tested on the COCHITO WPB-87329. No other CG vessels are so fitted.

USCGC Eagle

SAIL TRAINING SHIP

Ship	Pennant Number	Completion Date	Builder
EAGLE	WIX-327	1936	Blohm & Voss

Machinery One Caterpillar D399 auxiliary diesel; 1 shaft **Displacement** 1,816 tons **Dimensions** 70.4/89.5m x 12m x 4.9m **Sail Area** 25,351 ft **Speed** 10.5 knots (18 under sail) **Complement** 12 Officers; 38 Crew; 150 Cadets

Notes

A three-masted sailing Barque built in 1936 by the Blohm & Voss Shipyard, Hamburg, Germany, as a training vessel for German Naval Cadets. It was commissioned HORST WESSEL and following World War II was taken as a war prize by the United States. On May 15, 1946, the barque was commissioned into US Coast Guard service as the EAGLE and sailed from Bremerhaven, Germany to New London, Connecticut. She serves as a seagoing classroom for approximately 175 cadets and instructors from the U.S. Coast Guard Academy. When at home, EAGLE rests alongside a pier at the Coast Guard Academy on the Thames River.

USCGC Aspen

SEAGOING BUOY TENDERS
JUNIPER CLASS

Ship	Pennant Number	Completion Date	Builder
JUNIPER	201	1996	Marinette Marine
WILLOW	202	1996	Marinette Marine
KUKUI	203	1997	Marinette Marine
ELM	204	1998	Marinette Marine
WALNUT	205	1999	Marinette Marine
SPAR	206	2001	Marinette Marine
MAPLE	207	2001	Marinette Marine
ASPEN	208	2001	Marinette Marine
SYCAMORE	209	2002	Marinette Marine
CYPRESS	210	2002	Marinette Marine
OAK	211	2002	Marinette Marine
HICKORY	212	2003	Marinette Marine
FIR	213	2003	Marinette Marine
HOLLYHOCK	214	2003	Marinette Marine

Ship	Pennant Number	Completion Date	Builder
SEQUOIA	215	2004	Marinette Marine
ALDER	216	2004	Marinette Marine

Machinery Two Caterpillar 3608 diesels; 1 shaft **Displacement** 2,064 tons **Dimensions** 68.6m x 14m x 4m **Speed** 15 knots **Armament** 2 x 12.7 MG **Complement** 40

Notes

In 1993 the USCG awarded Marinette Marine a contract to construct the first of a new class of Sea-going Buoy Tenders to replace WWII era vessels. They are equipped with a single controllable pitch propeller, bow and stern thrusters which give the ship the maneuverability it needs to tend buoys offshore and in restricted waters. A Sophisticated Machinery Plant Control and Monitoring System and an Electronic Chart Display and Information System enable these vessels to reduce the watch standing complement compared to older cutters. A Dynamic Positioning System can hold the vessel within a 10 metre circle using the Global Positioning System allowing the crew to service and position floating aids to navigation more efficiently than before in winds to 30 knots and 8 foot seas. They are also ice-capable with the ability to break ice up to 14-inches thick at 3 knots or 3ft by ramming. In addition to the traditional tasks of tending to navigation markers these vessels have a limited salvage and oil-spill recovery capability.

USCGC Frank Drew

COASTAL BUOY TENDERS
KEEPER CLASS

Ship	Pennant Number	Completion Date	Builder
IDA LEWIS	551	1996	Marinette Marine
KATHERINE WALKER	552	1996	Marinette Marine
ABBIE BURGESS	553	1996	Marinette Marine
MARCUS HANNA	554	1996	Marinette Marine
JAMES RANKIN	555	1996	Marinette Marine
JOSHUA APPLEYBY	556	1996	Marinette Marine
FRANK DREW	557	1996	Marinette Marine
ANTHONY PETIT	558	1996	Marinette Marine
BARBARA MARBRITY	559	1996	Marinette Marine
WILLIAM TATE	560	1996	Marinette Marine
HARRY CLAIBORNE	561	1996	Marinette Marine
MARIA BRAY	562	1996	Marinette Marine

Ship	Pennant Number	Completion Date	Builder
HENRY BLAKE	563	1996	Marinette Marine
GEORGE COBB	564	1996	Marinette Marine

Machinery Two Caterpillar 3508TA diesels; 2 Ulstein Z-drives; bow thruster **Displacement** 840 tons FL **Dimensions** 53.3m x 11m x 2.4m **Speed** 12 knots **Complement** 18

Notes

Keeper Class tenders are tasked with maintaining aids to navigation (ATON), search and rescue (SAR), law enforcement (LE), migrant interdiction, marine safety inspections, environmental protection and natural resources management. Keeper Class cutters have limited ice breaking capability. They are the first Coast Guard cutters equipped with Z-Drive propulsion units instead of the standard propeller and rudder configuration. They are designed to independently rotate 360 degrees. Combined with a thruster in the bow, they give the Keeper class cutters unmatched maneuverability.

USCGC Bluebell

INLAND BUOY TENDERS

Ship	Pennant Number	Comm Date	Builder
BLUEBELL	313	1944	Birchfield Boiler Co.
BUCKTHORN	642	1963	Mobile Ship Repair

Machinery Two Caterpillar diesels; 2 shafts **Displacement** 226 tons 174 (BLUEBELL) **Dimensions** 30.5m x 7.3m x 1.5m (BUCKTHORN draft 1.2m) **Speed** 11.9 knots **Complement** 15

Notes

Two vessels of similar design but different vintage, undertaking the same role, both operating as Inland Buoy Tenders, BLUEBELL being based at Portland, Oergon and BUCKTHORN at Sault Sainte Marie in Mississippi.

USCGC Elderberry

BAYBERRY CLASS

Ship	Pennant Number	Completion Date	Builder
BAYBERRY	65400	1954	Reliable Shipyard, Olympia
ELDERBERRY	65401	1954	Reliable Shipyard, Olympia

Machinery Two GM diesels; 2 shafts **Displacement** 70 tons full load **Dimensions** 19.8m x 5.2m x 1.2m **Speed** 10 knots **Complement** 8

Notes

Now well into their sixth decade of service these two vessels are responsible for the maintenance of navigational buoys on inland waterways. BAYBERRY is based at Seattle and ELDERBERRY at Petersburg, Alaska.

USCGC Saginaw

CONSTRUCTION TENDERS
PAMLICO CLASS

Ship	Pennant Number	Completion Date	Builder
PAMLICO	800	1976	CG Yard, Curtis Bay Md
HUDSON	801	1976	CG Yard, Curtis Bay Md
KENNEBEC	802	1977	CG Yard, Curtis Bay Md
SAGINAW	803	1977	CG Yard, Curtis Bay Md

Machinery Two Caterpillar diesels; 2 shafts **Displacement** 39,400 tons **Dimensions** 249.9m x 31.8m x 7.9m **Speed** 24 knots **Complement** 14

Notes

Designed to place and repair aids to navigation (ATON) these vessels operate in by areas along the Gulf coast and Atlantic. As an example of the scale of the task, PAMLICO, which is based in New Orleans has an area of responsibility that covers 130 miles of coastline and 250 miles inland up the Mississippi river comprising 1200 navigational aids. Unlike other classes of construction tenders these vessels have an extended forecastle and working deck rather than the more usual pusher tug/barge combination. They are equipped with a 9-ton crane. HUDSON is based at Miami Beach, Florida; KENNEBEC at Portmouth, Virginia and SAGINAW at Mobile, Alabama.

USCGC Smilax

COSMOS CLASS

Ship	Pennant Number	Completion Date	Builder
SMILAX	315	1944	Dubuque Boat & Boiler

Machinery Two boilers; one geared steam turbines driving one shaft; 22,000shp **Displacement** 18,874 tons **Dimensions** 190m x 32m x 8.8m **Speed** 23 knots **Armament** 2 x Phalanx CIWS **Complement** 842

Notes

Reclassified from a WLI in 1979, SMILAX is one of the oldest vessels still in USCG service. She is based at Atlantic Beach, North Carolina, and pushes a 70-foot construction barge equipped with a 5-ton crane.

USCGC Anvil

ANVIL CLASS

Ship	Pennant Number	Comm Date	Builder
ANVIL	75301	1962	Gibbs Corporation, Jacksonville
HAMMER	75302	1962	Gibbs Corporation, Jacksonville
SLEDGE	75303	1962	McDermott Fabricators, Morgan City
MALLET	75304	1963	McDermott Fabricators, Morgan City
VISE	75305	1963	McDermott Fabricators, Morgan City
CLAMP	75306	1964	Sturgeon Bay SB & DD, Wisconsin
WEDGE	75307	1964	Sturgeon Bay SB & DD, Wisconsin
HATCHET	75309	1966	Dorchester SB, New Jersey
AXE	75310	1966	Dorchester SB, New Jersey

Machinery Two Caterpillar diesels; 2 shafts **Displacement** 140 tons **Dimensions** 22.9m x 6.7m x 1.2m **Speed** 10 knots **Complement** 13

Notes

CLAMP, HATCHET and AXE are one foot longer than the rest of the class. The vessels can push both 68-foot and 84-foot construction barges. WEDGE is now operated as a River Tender (WLR).

USCGC Greenbrier

RIVER TENDERS
GASCONADE CLASS

Ship	Pennant Number	Completion Date	Builder
GASCONADE	75401	1964	St Louis SB & DD
MUSKINGUM	75402	1965	Maxon Construction Co
WYACONDA	75403	1965	Maxon Construction Co
CHIPPEWA	75404	1965	Maxon Construction Co
CHEYENNE	75405	1966	Maxon Construction Co
KICKAPOO	75406	1969	Halter Marine, New Orleans
KANAWHA	75407	1969	Halter Marine, New Orleans
PATOKA	75408	1970	Halter Marine, New Orleans
CHENA	75409	1970	Halter Marine, New Orleans
KANKAKEE	75500	1990	Avondale Industries
GREENBRIER	75501	1990	Avondale Industries

Machinery Two Caterpillar diesels; 2 shafts **Displacement** 150 tons **Dimensions** 22.9m x 6.7m x 7m **Speed** 9 knots **Complement** 13

Notes

WLRs push barges equipped with cranes which work Aids To Navigation (ATON). Some are equipped with "jetting" devices which are used to set and anchor buoys in rivers with sandy/muddy bottoms. The barges are an integral part of ATON. Barge Lengths vary: 90 feet, 99 feet and 130 feet.

The tenders themselves are flat-ended and all operate on the Mississippi and its tributaries. KANKAKEE and GREENBRIER were approved under the 1986 budget and ordered in 1988. They act as push tugs for barges 74 and 75.

USCGC Osage

OUACHITA CLASS

Ship	Pennant Number	Completion Date	Builder
OUACHITA	65501	1960	Platzer SY Houston
CIMARRON	65502	1960	Platzer SY Houston
OBION	65503	1962	Gibbs Corp Jacksonville
SCIOTO	65504	1962	Gibbs Corp Jacksonville
OSAGE	65505	1962	Gibbs Corp Jacksonville
SANGAMON	65506	1962	Gibbs Corp Jacksonville

Machinery Two Caterpillar diesels; 2 shafts **Displacement** 146 tons **Dimensions** 19.8m x 6.4m x 0.4m **Speed** 10 knots **Complement** 13

Notes

All have an onboard 3-ton crane and operate on the Mississippi and its tributaries. The construction barges for each class are all numbered and assigned to specific vessels.

USCGC Thunder Bay

ICEBREAKING TUGS
BAY CLASS

Ship	Pennant Number	Commission Date	Builder
KATMAI BAY	101	1979	Tacoma Boatbuilding
BRISTOL BAY	102	1979	Tacoma Boatbuilding
MOBILE BAY	103	1979	Tacoma Boatbuilding
BISCAYNE BAY	104	1979	Tacoma Boatbuilding
NEAH BAY	105	1980	Tacoma Boatbuilding
MORRO BAY	106	1981	Tacoma Boatbuilding
PENOBSCOT BAY	107	1984	Bay City Marine
THUNDER BAY	108	1985	Bay City Marine
STURGEON BAY	109	1988	Bay City Marine

Machinery Diesel-Electric; 2 Fairbanks-Morse DG; 2 Westinghouse electric drive; 1 shaft **Displacement** 662 tons **Dimensions** 42.7m x 11.4m x 3.8m **Speed** 14.7 knots **Complement** 17

Notes

Icebreakers used primarily for domestic ice breaking duties. They are named after American Bays and are stationed mainly in Northeast US and Great Lakes. They use a low-pressure-air bubbler system that forces air and water between the hull and ice to reduce resistance and improve icebreaking capability. BRISTOL BAY & MOBILE BAY are augmented by a 120ft work barge for maintaining aids to navigation.

USCGC Hawser

HARBOUR TUGS SMALL
CAPSTAN CLASS

Ship	Pennant Number	Comm Date	Builder
CAPSTAN	65601	1961	Gibbs Corporation, Jacksonville
CHOCK	65602	1962	Gibbs Corporation, Jacksonville
TACKLE	65604	1962	Gibbs Corporation, Jacksonville
BRIDLE	65607	1963	Barbour Boat, New Bern. NC
PENDANT	65608	1963	Barbour Boat, New Bern. NC
SHACKLE	65609	1963	Barbour Boat, New Bern. NC
HAWSER	65610	1963	Barbour Boat, New Bern. NC
LINE	65611	1963	Barbour Boat, New Bern. NC
WIRE	65612	1963	Barbour Boat, New Bern. NC
BOLLARD	65614	1967	Western Boat Building Corp
CLEAT	65615	1967	Western Boat Building Corp

Machinery One Caterpillar 3412TA diesel; One shaft **Displacement** 72 tons **Dimensions** 19.8m x 8.5m x 2.1m **Speed** 10 knots **Complement** 6

Notes

Built between 1962 and 1967, they are employed only on the east coast, from Maine to Virginia. They routinely conduct aids to navigation, domestic ice operations, search and rescue and law enforcement duties.

MLB 47242

47' MOTOR LIFE BOAT (MLB)

Built by Textron Marine, the 47' motor lifeboat is designed as a first response rescue resource in high seas, surf & heavy weather environments. They are built to withstand the most severe conditions at sea and are capable of effecting a rescue at sea even under the most difficult circumstances. They are self-bailing, self-righting, almost unsinkable, and have a long cruising radius for their size. It is the replacement for the aging 44' MLB fleet.

As of 2010 there are 117 operational, being added to monthly. The total (to be delivered over 5 years) will be about 200.

41365 U.S. COAST GUARD

UTB 41365

41' UTILITY BOAT (UTB)

The 41' UTB is the general workhorse at multi-mission units. It is designed to operate under moderate weather and sea conditions where its speed and maneuverability make it an ideal platform for a variety of missions.

There are presently 172 operational boats.

RB-M 45601

45' RESPONSE BOAT MEDIUM (RB-M)

The Response Boat-Medium (RB-M) replaces the ageing fleet of 41' Utility Boats (UTB with improvements in performance, crew efficiency and operational availability.

The RB-M is intended to conduct a broad range of vital Coast Guard missions, including homeland security, search and rescue, and law enforcement.

To date 31 vessels have been delivered to the Coast Guard out of a scheduled requirement for 180 RB-M.

36' LONG RANGE INTERCEPTOR (LRI)

Displacement 24,000 lbs **Length** 11 metres **Machinery** Two diesel engines; water jet propulsion **Capacity** 14 personnel; 150lbs of equipment **Speed** 45 knots **Range** 400 nm **Endurance** 10 hours **Armament** M240 7.62mm general purpose machine gun

Notes

Intended to be carried by the new Bertholf class, up to three can be accommodated and operated at any one time. Major cutters will be assigned an LRI, equipped with radar, data links and over-the-horizon navigation and communication equipment to operate as an interceptor. Built by Willard Marine and Integrated Coast Guard Systems it is planned to acquire up to 33 boats.

ANB 55105

21-64' AID TO NAVIGATION BOATS

The USCG maintains roughly 145 Aids to Navigation Boats of varying size and capability, too numerous to list individually in a book of this size.

In the main, these boats were designed primarily to operate within the inland waters of the United States. However the 55' ANB is often employed to service offshore aids as well.

The 55' ANB has a crane that is used for hoisting and securing the various buoys and aids to navigation that the Coast Guard supplies for waterways. Most Aids to Navigation Boats of the USCG are stationed at Station - Aids to Navigation (STANTs). These serve as joint Law Enforcement, Search and Rescue, and Aids to Navigation stations.

Most USCG boats (everything below 65-feet is classified as a boat, rather than a cutter or tender, in USCG parlance) carry a five or six digit pennant number in place of a name. The first two characters of which signify the vessel's length in feet.

25' TRANSPORTABLE PORT SECURITY BOAT (TPSB)

Also known as the Guardian, this vessel is a twin outboard motor, open deck, all weather, high performance craft based on the proven Boston Whaler design. It is capable of operating in inner harbour or near shore environments in light sea conditions. First built in 1997 by Boston Whaler in Edgewater, Florida, for the USCG, TPSB is designed and configured to support Port Security Units in surface interdiction. The TPSB is outfitted as a military gunboat with three hardened weapon positions; one forward capable of mounting a .50 caliber (12.7mm) tri-pod and two pintles, situated one on either side capable of mounting a 7.62 mm M240B Machine Gun.

25658

25' DEFENDER CLASS (RB-HS/RB-S)

The Response Boat-Small was developed in a direct response to the need for additional Homeland Security assets in the wake of the 9/11 terrorist attacks. The Defender-class boats were procured under an emergency acquisition authority. With a contract option for up to 500 standard response boats (470 for Coast Guard, 20 for Department of Homeland Security and 10 for US Navy), the Defender-class acquisition is one of the largest boat acquisitions of its type in the world.

Deliveries of the 100 Defender A-class (RB-HS) began in May 2002 and continued until August 2003. A follow-on Defender B-class (RB-S) included a longer cabin and shock mounted seats. The first were delivered in October 2003, and there are now 450 Defender-class boats in operation assigned to the Coast Guard's Maritime Safety and Security Teams (MSST), Maritime Security Response Team (MSRT), Marine Safety Units (MSU), and Small Boat Stations throughout the Coast Guard.

US COAST GUARD AVIATION

The US Coast Guard uses a variety of platforms to conduct its daily business. Cutters and small boats are used on the water and fixed and rotary wing (helicopter) aircraft are used in the air.

There are a total of 211 aircraft in Coast Guard inventory. This figure fluctuates operationally due to maintenance schedules. Major Missions include Search and Rescue, Law Enforcement, Environmental Response, Ice Operations, and Air Interdiction. Fixed-wing aircraft such as the C-130 Hercules, HU-25 Falcon jets and now the HC-144A Ocean Sentry, operate from large and small Air Stations. Rotary wing aircraft (H-65 Dolphin and HH-60 Jayhawk helicopters) operate from flight-deck equipped Cutters, Air Stations and Air Facilities.

Type	Number Operational	Number in storage	Total
HC-144A Ocean Sentry	10		Plans to acquire 36
HC-130J Hercules	6		6
HC-130H Hercules	22	5	27
It is intended to convert at least 16 HC-130H to operate alongside the HC-130J in the Long Range Surveillance role			
HU-25 Guardian	20	21	41
HH-60 Jayhawk	35	7	42
It is intended to convert all HH-60 Jayhawk aircraft to MH-60T Medium Range Recovery Helicopter standard.			
H-65 Dolphin	90	12	102
It is intended to convert all H-65 Dolphin aircraft to MCH-65 Multi-mission Cutter Helicopter standard.			

EADS/CASA HC-144A

Variants HC-144A
Role Medium Range Surveillance aircraft
Engines Two General Electric CT7-93C Turboprop engines.
Length 21.4 metres **Height** 8.18 metres **Wingspan** 25.81 metres
Speed 236 knots **Ceiling** 30,000+ feet
Range 1,565 nautical miles.
Crew Minimum Two **Endurance** 8.7 hours

Notes

Employed to perform homeland security and search and rescue missions, enforce laws and treaties including illegal drug interdiction, marine environmental protection, military readiness, and international ice patrol missions, as well as cargo and personnel transport. The size, range and reconfiguration capabilities make this a versatile aircraft. Equipped with a Rockwell-Collins Flight 2 glass cockpit instrument panel, autopilot & avionics suite for a two-person aircrew.
Able to embark a mission equipment pallet, interoperable with that of the HC-130J long-range surveillance aircraft and includes C4ISR equipment for enhanced situational awareness; improved surveillance through radar and electro-optical/infrared sensors systems; mission data recording; a first-responder/law enforcement and marine communications suite and enhanced secure data encryption capabilities. It is planned to acquire 36 aircraft to eventually replace the HU-25 Guardian.

Lockheed HC-130 HERCULES

Variants HC-130H; HC-130J
Role Long Range Surveillance aircraft
Engines Four Allison T56-A15 turboprop engines (Allison AE2100D3 in HC-130J).
Length 29.8 metres **Height** 11.6 metres **Wingspan** 40.4 metres
Speed 330 knots (350 knots HC-130J). **Ceiling** 33,000+ feet
Range 4,100 nautical miles (5,500 nautical miles HC-130J).
Crew Seven
Endurance 14 hours (21 hours HC-130J)

Notes

The USCG operates 27 HC-130H aircraft from five bases around the United States. They are used for search and rescue, enforcement of laws and treaties, illegal drug interdiction, marine environmental protection, military readiness, International Ice Patrol missions, as well as cargo and personnel transport. The service also currently operates an additional 6 HC-130J aircraft from CGAS Elizabeth City. It is also modernising sixteen of the older C-130Hs to meet long range maritime patrol requirements in areas (such as the Pacific Ocean) that cannot be patrolled efficiently by medium range surveillance aircraft or cutters.

Dassault HU-25 GUARDIAN

Variants HU-25A; HU-25B; HU-25C
Role Medium Range Surveillance aircraft
Engines Two Garrett ATF3-6-2C Turbofans.
Length 17.15 metres **Height** 5.32 metres **Wingspan** 16.3 metres
Speed 465 knots **Ceiling** 42,000 feet
Range 1,808 nautical miles
Crew Two

Notes

Based on the Dassault Falcon 20 business jet the USCG acquired the aircraft to replace the HU-16E Albatross. It operates the aircraft in three variants, the primary difference being in the installed sensor package. The HU-25A is the standard MRS version. The HU-25B is a pollution control variant fitted with side-looking airborne radar (SLAR) while the HU-25C is a drug interdiction variant equipped with a Westinghouse APG-66 search radar and WF-360 infra-red turret. The current fleet comprises 25 HU-25As (16 of which are in storage); 7 HU-25Bs (4 in storage) and 9 HU-25Cs (1 in storage).

Eurocopter H-65 DOLPHIN

Variants H-65B; H-65C; MCH-65
Role Short Range Recovery helicopter
Engines Two Turbomeca Arriel 2C2-CG turboshaft engines.
Length 11.6 metres **Height** 4.0 metres **Rotor Diameter** 11.9 metres
Speed 165 knots. **Ceiling** 15,000 feet
Range 350 - 410 nautical miles.
Crew Two pilots and two crew.
Armament One 7.62 MG and one .50 cal precision rifle

Notes

There are now a total of 102 Dolphins in the Coast Guard Fleet. The fleet has home ports in 17 cities on the Atlantic and Pacific Oceans, Gulf of Mexico, Hawaii, and the Great Lakes region. The helicopter is usually deployed from shore but it can be deployed from medium and high endurance Coast Guard Cutters, as well as the Polar Icebreakers. The H-65C upgrade began in 2004 and includes an upgraded main gear-box and tail gearbox, a longer nose to house avionics and an increased maximum take-off weight. The aircraft are now undergoing an upgrade to MCH-65 standard enabling them to perform SAR, law enforcement and Homeland Security missions. Re-engining will provide 40% more power and higher performance. The upgrade will also include enhanced C4ISR equipment; improved vertical insertion and vertical delivery capability - the ability to deliver a 3-person interagency counter-terrorism or response team 50 nm from a US shore or a Coast Guard flight deck equipped cutter and eim-proved radar and electro-optical sensors. Weapons will also be fitted to allow warning shots and disabling fire should they be required.

Sikorsky HH-60J JAYHAWK

Variants HH-60J; MH-60T
Role Medium Range Recovery Helicopter
Engines Two General Electric T700-401C gas turbines.
Length 19.76 metres **Height** 5.18metres **Rotor Diameter** 16.36 metres
Speed 180 knots **Ceiling** 5,000 feet
Range 700 nautical miles.
Crew Pilot; Co-pilot and two flight crew.
Armament One 7.62 mm M240H medium MG in starboard door (MH-60T)
One 12.7 mm Barrett semi-automatic rifle (MH-60T)

Notes

HH-60J is a variant of the ubiquitous UH-60 Blackhawk family of helicopters of which 42 were delivered to the USCG between 1990 and 1996. They can be deployed onboard USCG cutters and in the SAR role can accommodate up to six survivors.
The MH-60T Medium Range Recovery Helicopter upgrade programme began in 2007 and is scheduled to provide upgraded avionics and operational capabilities to all 42 existing HH-60J airframes by 2015. This will provide a glass cockpit, an enhanced elec-tro-optic/infrared sensor system as well as a radar sensor system and airborne use of force capability which includes both weapons for firing warning and disabling shots and armour to protect the aircrew from small arms fire. As each airframe upgrade is com-pleted, the affected HH-60J will be re-designated to MH-60T.

GLOSSARY

The military throughout the world have a passion for acronyms and abbreviations - and the US Armed Forces are no exception. Any modern day reference book will be liberally scattered with these, sometimes annoying, abbreviations - second nature to those in the know, but frustrating for the general reader. The following pages should help you through some of the 'alphabet soup' that will inevitably be found in this volume.

AAG	Advanced Arresting Gear	DSRV	Deep Submergence Recovery Vehicle
ABM	Anti-ballistic Missile		
ADCAP	Advanced Capability	EB	General Dynamics (Electric Boat)
AEM/S	Advanced Enclosed Mast/Sensor		
		EFV	Expeditionary Fighting Vehicle
ANB	Aids to Navigation Boats		
ARG	Amphibious Ready Group	EMALS	Electro Magnetic Aircraft Launch System
ARS	Auxiliary Rescue and Salvage Vessel		
		EMNS	Expendable Mine Neutralization System
AS	Submarine Depot Ship		
ASROC	Anti-submarine Rocket	ESG	Expeditionary Strike Group
ASW	Anti-submarine Warfare		
ATON	Aids to Navigation	ESSM	Evolved Sea Sparrow Missile
CEC	Co-operative Engagement Capability		
		EW	Electronic Warfare
C4ISR	Command, Control, Communications, Computers, Intelligence, Surveillance and Reconnaissance	FFG	Frigate (Guided Missile)
		FL	Full Load
		FLIR	Forward Looking Infra-Red
		FRC	Fast Response Cutter
		FRP	Fleet Response Plan
CG	Cruiser	FSF	Fast Sea Frame
CG(X)	Cruiser (Next Generation)	FSS	Fast Sealift Ship
CIWS	Close In Weapon System	GD	General Dynamics
COTS	Commercial Off The Shelf	GE	General Electric
CSG	Carrier Strike Group	GTS	Gas Turbine Ship
CVBG	Carrier Battle Group	HM	Helicopter Mine Countermeasures Squadron
CV	Aircraft Carrier		
CVN	Aircraft Carrier (Nuclear)		
CVW	Carrier Air Wing	HMH	USMC Heavy Helicopter Squadron
DDG	Destroyer (Guided Missile)		

HMLA	USMC Light Attack Helicopter Squadron	LPD	Landing Ship, Personnel, Dock
HMM	USMC Medium Helicopter Squadron	LRI	Long Range Interceptor
		LSD	Landing Ship, Dock
HMMT	USMC Heavy Helicopter Training Squadron	LST	Landing Ship, Tank
		LSV	Large Scale Vessel
HMT	USMC Helicopter Training Squadron	MARAD	Maritime Administration
		MAW	USMC Air Wing
HSC	Helicopter Sea Combat Squadron	MCAS	Marine Corps Air Station
		MCDS	Modular Cargo Delivery Syetem
HSM	Helicopter Maritime Strike Squadron	MCM	Mine Countermeasures Vessel
HSV	High Speed Vessel		
HT	Helicopter Training Squadron	MCS	Mine Warfare Command and Support Vessel
IBU	Inshore Boat Unit	MEF	Marine Expeditionary Force
ICBM	Inter Continental Ballistic Missile		
		MG	Machine Gun
JPATS	Joint Primary Air Training System	MHC	Coastal Minesweeper
		MIRV	Multiple Independently Targeted Re-entry Vehicles
LASH	Lighter Aboard Ship		
LCAC	Landing Craft (Air Cushion)		
		MLB	Motor Life Boat
LCC	Amphibious Command and Control Ship	MLE	Mission Life Extension
		MMA	Multi-mission Maritime Aircraft
LCS	Littoral Combat Ship		
LCU	Landing Craft (Utility)	MPF	Maritime Pre-positioning Force
LFA	Low Frequency Array		
LHA	Landing Ship, Helicopter Assault	MPF(F)	Maritime Pre-positioning Force (Future)
LHA(R)	Landing Ship, Helicopter Assault (Replacement)	MPS	Maritime Pre-positioning Squadron
LHD	Landing Ship Helicopter, Dock	MSC	Military Sealift Command
		MSST	Maritime Safety and Security Team
LKA	Landing Ship, Attack, Cargo		
		MSRT	Maritime Security Response Team
LM	Lockheed Martin		
LMSR	Large, Medium Speed Ro-Ro	MSU	Marine Safety Unit
		MT	Motor Tanker

MV	Merchant Vessel	SSN	Attack Submarine (Nuclear Powered)
NAB	Naval Amphibious Base		
NAS	Naval Air Station	SSBN	Ballistic Missile Submarine (Nuclear Powered)
NAVSEA	Naval Sea Systems Command		
NAWC	Naval Air Warfare Centre	SSGN	Cruise Missile Submarine (Nuclear Powered)
NCWRON	Naval Coastal Warfare Squadron		
		SSV	Submarine Support Vessel
NDRF	National Defence Reserve Force	SURTASS	Surface Towed Array System
NFAF	Naval Fleet Auxiliary Force	SWATH	Small Waterplane Twin Hull
		SY	Shipyard
NGNN	Northrop Grumman Newport News	TACAMO	Take Charge & Move Out
		TACTOM	Tactical Tomahawk
NGSS	Northrop Grumman Ship Systems	T-ACS	Auxiliary Crane Ship
		T-AE	Auxiliary Ammunition Ship
NSC	National Security Cutter	T-AFS	Auxiliary Combat Stores Ship
OPC	Offshore Patrol Cutter		
OPDS	Offshore Petroleum Distribution System	T-AGF	Auxiliary Command Ship
		T-AGM	Auxiliary Range Instrumentation Ship
OPEVAL	Operational Evaluation		
PC	Patrol Craft	T-AGOR	Auxiliary Acoustic Survey Ship
PPIP	Planned Product Improvement Programme		
		T-AGOS	Auxiliary Ocean Surveillance Ship
PRM	Pressurized Rescue Module	T-AGS	Auxiliary Oceonographic Survey Ship
RAM	Rolling Airframe Missile		
RB-M	Response Boat - Medium	T-AH	Auxiliary Hospital Ship
RCS	Rescue Capable System	T-AKE	Auxiliary Dry Cargo Ship
RO-RO	Roll On - Roll Off	T-AK	Auxiliary Transport, Container
RRF	Ready Reserve Fleet		
SALM	Single Anchor Leg Moor	T-AKR	Auxiliary Transport, Ro-Ro
SB	Shipbuilder	T-AO	Auxiliary Fleet Replenishment Oiler
SEAL	Sea Air and Land (USN Special Forces)		
		T-AOT	Auxiliary Transport Tanker
SLEP	Service Life Extension Programme	T-AOE	Auxiliary Fast Combat Support Ship
SRDRS	Submarine Rescue Diving and Compression System	T-ARC	Auxiliary Cable Repair Ship
		T-AVB	Auxiliary Aviation Logistics Ship
SS	Steam Ship		

T-ARS	Auxiliary Rescue and Salvage Ship	VOO	Vessel of Opportunity
T-ATF	Auxiliary Fleet Tug	VP	Maritime Patrol Squadron
TPSB	Transportable Port Security Boat	VQ	Special Warfare Squadron
		VR	Transport Squadron
USCG	US Coast Guard	VRC	Composite Transport Squadron
USMC	US Marine Corps	VS	Anti-Submarine Squadron
USNS	United States Naval Ship	V/STOL	Vertical/Short Take-off or Landing
USS	United States Ship		
UTB	Utility Boat	VT	Training Squadron
VAW	Airborne Early Warning Squadron	VX	Trials Squadron
		WAGB	Icebreaker
VAQ	Electronic Warfare Squadron	WHEC	High Endurance Cutter
		WLB	Seagoing Buoy Tender
VFA	Fighter Attack Squadron	WLBB	Seagoing Buoy Tender Icebreaker
VLS	Vertical Launch System		
VMA	USMC Attack Squadron	WLI	Inland Buoy Tender
VMAQ	USMC Electronic Warfare Squadron	WLIC	Inland Construction Tender
		WLM	Coastal Buoy Tender
VMFA	USMC Fighter Attack Squadron	WLR	River Buoy Tender
		WMEC	Medium Endurance Cutter
VMFA(AW)	USMC Fighter Attack Squadron (All Weather)	WMSL	Maritime Security Cutter (Large)
VMFT	USMC Fighter Training Squadron	WPB	Patrol Boat
		WPC	Patrol Boat Coastal
VMGR	USMC Tanker/Transport Squadron	WTGB	Icebreaking Tug
		WYTL	Small Harbour Tug
VMM	USMC Tilt Rotor Squadron		